Henry Root, who made a fortune in wet fish, has spent the past ten years in correspondence with powerful and famous people across Britain. His sensible and firmly expressed views have made him the Lord Chesterfield of his time.

Apart from the original *Henry Root Letters*, Mr Root has published the *World of Knowledge* and the *A to Z of Women*. There are those who have called Henry Root a fraud, a phoney or a bonehead. On the other hand, many feel he stands for all that is truly British amid today's declining standards. Most of all, Henry Root is unignorable.

By the same author

Henry Root Letters
World of Knowledge
A to Z of Women

HENRY ROOT

The Soap Letters

GRAFTON BOOKS

A Division of the Collins Publishing Group

LONDON GLASGOW
TORONTO SYDNEY AUCKLAND

Grafton Books
A Division of the Collins Publishing Group
8 Grafton Street, London W1X 3LA

Published by Grafton Books 1989

First published in Great Britain by
Michael O'Mara Books Ltd 1988

Copyright © 1988 Henry Root

A CIP catalogue record for this book is
available from the British Library

ISBN 0-586-20801-1

Printed and bound in Great Britain

Set in Times

139 Elm Park Mansions
Park Walk
London, SW10.

Mr 'Tiny' Rowland
Lonrho plc
Cheapside
London, EC2.

27th March 1987.

Dear 'Tiny',

    Some damn fool publishers have commissioned me to write a book on money. I don't know about money. I thought I did but the world's moved on since I made my pile. I used the knuckle and stood up close, I breathed on the back of their necks. They didn't like that, they did a runner leaving me with their high street leases. A large man moving at speed, my fist a blur in the gathering night - that was my way. 17½ stone on the hoof. Not a pretty sight, but most effective.

    It's all changed now. Big bangs, tactical back-scratching, shredding-machines, 'unusual payments', teenage commodity millionaires with Porsche and Filofax as taut as piano-wire on so-called 'crack', Sir Saunders of Boots (or was it Burton's?) caught in his half-hose with a topless 'model', my pal Archer paying Irish tarts to leave the country - I don't have to tell you.

    Is all this necessary? Is this the modern way of doing things? I have recently had my staff urine-sampled as per instructions from the Home Office and not one of them was crack-positive, least of all myself. Is this why I'm out of it, why I received no invite to Lord Weidenfeld's Christmas do - hardly an Everest for social climbers, I think you'll agree. I pitched up anyway, mixed with buffs and spongers in slip-on shoes and velvet flippers, tried to dance with Geoffrey Wheatcroft. 'Je suis contre,' he said. I was ejaculated in my pumps.

    Plus they turn down my concepts, 'Tiny', they ignore my letters. I wrote recently to the Polite Society and they didn't fucking answer. I've written to Thatcher, to Twyford Toilets, to Bob Monkhouse and 'The Price Is Right', supplied innuendoes to the BBC - nothing! I'm old and I'm tired and my legs have turned blue. The boy's on the game, the girl's on drugs and Mrs Root's gone off with Bath's boy, Weymouth, who wears a frock and lives up a tree. Mrs Root recently had her face lifted and now she looks like Burt Lancaster, so Weymouth can't be spoilt for choice.

    Can you help me? Can you give me a job? For pity's sake answer.

    I'm at the crossroads here, I tell you.

Henry Root

Henry Root.

139 Elm Park Mansions
Park Walk
London, SW10.

19th March 1987.

The Chairman
Twyfords Toilets
Basingstoke
Hampshire.

Dear Sir or Madam,

You will have heard of the Booker Prize for fiction, sponsored by McConnel plc, whereby, amid publicity accruing to McConnel, a little Jap or Maori novelist hits the jackpot with a book which no one reads, least of all the judges. Nothing wrong with that.

How about a Twyfords Toilets Prize for toilet books, a genre thus designated since they are intended for browsing while at stool? I suggest a panel of judges chosen for their expertise in this field, themselves writers of toilet books, viz: Jimmy Riddle, Miles Kington, Arthur Marshall, Kenneth Williams, Gyles Brandreth, Bill Oddie and Maureen Lipman. The prize, as well as money, could be a bronze of Maureen Lipman wearing a comical expression on the john.

I take it you're a Tory, sir? I ask since I have a second proposition and it seems wise to check first that you favour the modern way of doing things in Mrs Thatcher's self-help Britain. Here's the dodge: I am myself a toilet book writer of some res- ource, having no less that eight on sale this Xmas. We see to it that I win the prize _and_ _you_ _and_ _I_ trouser the money fifty-fifty, no questions asked. What do you say to that?

I would further confirm that within seconds of receipt your letter of concurrance will go through my shredder, the contents having been memorised. We don't keep files here, we've minds like lobster-pots.

Let's help ourselves to help ourselves!

Yours faithfully,

Henry Root

Henry Root.

Sir Ralph Halpern
Boots
8-11 Great Castle Street
London, W1.

139 Elm Park Mansions
Park Walk
London, SW10.

1st April 1987.

Dear Sir Ralph,

I'm in deep snooker here, old pal, I tell you frankly. I weigh 22 stone, I can't see my feet and Mrs Root's gone off with Bath's boy Weymouth. Can't blame her, I suppose. For the most part I ignored her. She pleased me once. I can see her now with bouffant hair and cocktail frock sitting on a bar-stool at Les Amies Sportifes. I gathered her up and then ignored her. Too busy punching upwards. Never been much good with women - vis-a-vis women I'm on all fours with my friend Max Hastings, who sits in combat pants in icy puddles hardening his resolve and then expects his dinner to be ready. My method with women was to bear down on them suddenly, to grip them from behind and put my hand inside their clothes. Seldom worked, never in fact. Last night, after Cod Florentine by Findus (cooked in the bag - and, in error, in the washing-machine), I found myself watching 'Terry And June' on my own. Is this it? I thought. Is this the end? A man of a certain age watching 'Terry And June' on his own on a Friday night? I decided on the spot to come in henceforth at a different angle - charm, posture, rhythm, aplomb - to talk to women about themselves, about their operations, their intestinal gasses - that's what they like, is it not? Is this your method? Can you help? Can you advise? You know women from all I hear.

On top of which my concepts are ignored, my letters go un-answered. Today I wrote to Tom Maschler, temporarily with Cape, telling him I'd sold a TV concept to Michael Grade, and to Grade telling him I'd sold the concept of the book to Maschler. Silly thing to do. Neither is as stupid as he looks, both will see through the caper. I need a holiday, but can't afford it. I could bog off with primus stove and personal palliasse, no doubt, camping with others in the Dordogne area of France, not least Conque, but what would I do? Eat and reflect on La condition humaine as per Levin? Can't do that. Never been able to reflect. Too stupid, I suppose.

Plus I'm commissioned to write a book on money by some damn fool publishers and I'm stumped on this one too. Can you help, can you advise on this as well as women? They say that behind every rich man there's a great crime or a woman with nothing to wear. I gather you gave Miss Wright a charge-card, so she'll have been okay for lip-stick, suppositories etc. My charge card would render hallibut or worse. Can you help me with my book on money? Can you lend me twenty pounds? I enclose a tenner on account.

It will take a miracle now.

Yours on the ropes,

Henry Root.

THE BURTON GROUP PLC

CHAIRMAN'S OFFICE

26 May 1987

Henry Root Esq
139 Elm Park Mansions
Park Walk
London SW10

Dear Mr Root

Sir Ralph has asked me to reply to your very kind note of 7 April, and the enclosed gift.

He says, yes, he's sure he'd very much like to help you in your enquiries and wonders what he can do for you. Sadly, he doesn't have a fiver, but sends you back half of your original tenner* — we hope it's of some help.

Yours sincerely

Mary E Lally
PA to Sir Ralph Halpern

*The other half to follow next time.

8-11 GREAT CASTLE STREET · LONDON WIN 7AD · TELEPHONE · 01-927 0002 · TELEX 21484 · FAX 01-927 0580

The Burton Group plc Registered in England Company No. 237511 Registered Office: 214 Oxford Street, London WIN 9DF

139 Elm Park Mansions
Park Walk
London, SW10.

2nd April 1987.

Lord Hanson
The Hanson Trust
180 Brompton Road
London, SW3.

Dear Lord Hanson,

My friend Nigel Dempster recently 'revealed' in his column that you are taking on senior staff - viz Michael Shea ex of the Queen. According to Dempster, Shea landed the job thanks to a sense of humour. Dempster reported thus: '"The Derby?" Shea inimitably joked, "when's that!?"'

I don't think that's inimitable. The Grand National? When's that? The Two Thousand Guineas? When's that? The St Leger? When's that? I could go on.

I've suffered a reverse here, Hanson (no need to go into detail - to do with the loss of capital plus Mrs Root) and am in consequence considering re-employment after a life-time in fish. I would be grateful for an interview - with a sense of humour displayed, if you insist - at your earliest convenience.

I do not currently take drugs as per post Goodison's Big Bang etc and am unclear whether this is likely to count against me. Nor have I been involved in a scandal like my friend Sir Halpern of Boots, but this could be arranged, no doubt. Apropos, do you think it is permissable to pay one's debt to society before a scandal rather than when caught? Many who get their feet a little muddy - Profumo, Lambton, Parkinson etc - pay their debt to society once nailed, working in the East End and posing with their boot-faced wives outside country churches looking sheepish. The fact is, Hanson, I've done my bit in the East End already - it was three-to-the-shirt where I was born and the outside bucket - and I'm hoping that this could count as my time in the wilderness. What do you think? I'd embark on a scandal with an easier mind without the thought of the East End, boot-faced wives and country churches hanging over me.

I like your new adverts starring Glenda Jackson. Been in a fight, has she? The other fellow may look even worse, of course.

I look forward to hearing from you.

Yours up to here in it,

Henry Root

Henry Root.

Mr Henry Root
c/o Weidenfeld Ltd
94 Clapham High Street
London SW4.

'Rosewood'
Middleton-on-Sea
Sussex.

28th March 1987

Dear Mr Root,

I am an 81-year-old spinster living with
my widowed sister, Mabel, who is 86, and I
wanted to tell you how much we have enjoyed
your book 'Henry Root's World Of Knowledge'.
Whenever one of us is in the dumps we get out
your book and have a good chuckle.

In fact I'm a bit of a scribbler myself
(Mabel often jokes that in spite of her hip
and my leg she has her roses and I have my
scribbling!) and this is the other reason why
I'm writing to you. I've never had much success (none at all in fact! - 66 radio plays submitted and none performed!) but my scribbling
keeps me happy and now I think I may have had
quite a good idea.

Mabel and I don't get out too much, of course,
but we do read the papers and I have been much
struck recently by all the talk of declining
standards in the City of London, with all manner of deceit and drugs and so on - all a consequence, I suppose, of the wrong sort of people having the money these days. Wouldn't a
soap opera called 'The WestEnders' make a

pleasant change from that horrid 'EastEnders'
with all those common people and Dirty Den
shouting at one another? I have scribbled out
a story-line which involves two families - one
rich, one poor, one on the way up, the other
in decline - whose fates become intertwined
because the son of each family meet in the City
and both become corrupted by drugs and the new
money-making ethos. The privileged family,
which is quite exhausted, can do nothing, but
the father of the humble family takes matters
into his own hands, leading a one-man fight
against corruption.

What do you think? Could you, with your
connections, possibly bring it to the attention of the right people? I would be so grate-
ful if you could help. Mabel and I may have to sell our beloved Rosewood Cottage unless our fortunes change. Do
let me know if you would like to see the short
synopsis I have scribbled down.

I so much look forward to hearing from
you, Mr Root. Each morning now I will eager-
ly await the postman's knock!

Yours very sincerely,

Lucy M Kelly

139 Elm Park Mansions
Park Walk
London, SW10.

Miss Lucy Appleby   3rd April 1987.
Rosewood Cottage
Middleton-On-Sea
Sussex.

Dear Miss Appleby,

   Your letter of 28th March via my friend Lord Weidenfeld to
hand. Your kind remarks re my book 'HENRY ROOT'S WORLD OF KNOW-
LEDGE' are noted - though I am uncertain as to why it made you
chuckle. Thinkers such as Wheatcroft, Muggeridge and Irma Kurtz
take it to be a great modern reference work.

   'When you read a good book it should be like sitting next
to the author at an agreeable dinner-party'.

   What's funny about that?

   With regard to your own scribbling, I doubt if there is much
to be said for a TV soap entitled 'The WestEnders' at this time,
but it is hard to make a sound commercial judgement without first
reading it. If you would care to send me the short synopsis you
mention, together with a stamped addressed envelope for return of
same, I would be glad to sift and advise. Bearing in mind your
regrettable circumstances, I will charge you only half my custom-
ary reading fee of £50 plus postage.

   Yours sincerely,

   Henry Root

   Henry Root.

Mr Henry Root
139 Elm Park Mansions
Park Walk
London, SW10.

'Rosewood'
Middleton-on-Sea
Sussex.

4th April 1987.

Dear Mr Root,

Your kind letter of 3rd April bucked me
up no end, and I am more grateful to you than
I can say for agreeing to read the synopsis of
my little play. I enclose it now, with, as requested, a stamped addressed envelope, and I
can hardly wait for your reaction! Mabel and
I are both keeping our fingers crossed I can
tell you! Poor Mabel's hip is worse and she's
confined to bed at the moment, but your letter
was just the tonic she needed.

Thank you so much for your kindness.

Yours sincerely,

Lucy Appleby

Enc: 'The WestEnders' by Lucy Appleby.

---

139 Elm Park Mansions
Park Walk
London, SW10.

5th April 1987.

Ms Clare Ogilvie
Gordon & Ogilvie Ltd
22 Half Moon Street
London, W1.

Dear Ms Ogilvie,

Your name has been given to me by my friend the Duke of
Devonshire as a sensible person to approach re finance and casting
of TV soaps, having, as you do, Sir Brown of Aston Martins on the
board.

I enclose the synopsis of my TV development - THE WESTENDERS by
HENRY ROOT - for your assessment and would say that were you to
'persuade' Sir Brown to steer what we in the business call seed money
in my direction, then I would put the casting of the proprety your
way. What do you say to that?

I look forward to receiving your positive reaction.

Yours sincerely,

Henry Root

Henry Root.

Enc: THE WESTENDERS by HENRY ROOT.

H.R. PRODUCTIONS
Suites 9-57
139 Elm Park Mansions
Park Walk
London, SW10.

6th April 1987.

Major-General Wyldebore-Smith
Conservative Board of Finance
32 Smith Square
London, SW1P 3HH.

Dear Wyldebore-Smith,

You will recall our correspondence of '79 in which I offered the Tories a substantial cheque cash down, quite untraceable, no questions asked, in return for a title, baron upwards? You replied, courteously (though tongue in cheek, I take it), to the effect that it wasn't possible to buy a title from the Tories! Never mind. It was on and up without your help and sideways into art, not least TV developments. This time the boot is on the other foot, my old steeplechaser, and I intend to put my hand deep into your trousers.

Here's the size of it. I have commissioned myself to write and produce a TV series - THE WESTENDERS by HENRY ROOT - which will trace the sad decline of this once great country over the past 25 years. I will draw a connection between the loosening of moral imperatives during the so-called Sixties - the Trial of Lady Chatterley, the pill, Mary Quant, the Great Train Robbery, 'Ready Steady Let's Go!' (you will recall that when Mick Jagger, wearing a black lace body-stocking, first appeared on this, Mary Whitehouse hit the TV screen with a bolt of projectile vomit) - and today's scandals in the City of London and in the Tory Party under Mrs Thatcher (insider dealings, 'unusual payments', shredding-machines, my pal, Sir Halpern of Boots, caught in his half-hose with a topless 'model', Tory MPs in service flats drilling firm young men in army shorts - I don't have to tell you.)

I have budgeted the venture at a round £10 million and am offering the Tories ground-floor participation plus residuals (change rights, four-walling, Australia, T-shirts - I won't blind you with science) in return for not divulging on screen everything I know. It would look suspicious, would it not, were the Tories not to get four-square behind a project of such timeliness?

Mrs Whitehouse is in, of course, as are the Pope, the Bishop of London, James Anderton, that silly sod who runs the Conservative Family Campaign (Graham Stanley-Gardner?) and Lindy Benson.

I enclose my cheque in favour of yourself. You look after me and I'll look after you. Box on, my old turkey, it's the only way.

I still think you have a more sensible name than your under-strapper Brigadier H. Lee.

Yours for a venture,

Henry Root.

Henry Root.

CONSERVATIVE BOARD OF FINANCE

Chairman:
R. ALISTAIR McALPINE

Director:
MAJOR-GENERAL F.B. WYLDBORE-SMITH,
C.B., D.S.O., O.B.E.

Deputy Director
BRIGADIER L.H. LEE C.B.E.

32 SMITH SQUARE,
WESTMINSTER, SW1P 3HH

TELEPHONE: 01-222 9000

Henry Root Esq
H.R. Productions
139 Elm Park Mansions
Park Walk
London, SW10.   15th April 1987.

Dear Mr Root,

    Major-General Wyldbore-Smith has asked me to reply to your
letter of 6th April. He well remembers your offensive letters of
1979, with their ill-mannered references to his name and their erron-
eous assumption that honours can be bought from the Tories. He has
instructed me to repeat what he said on that occasion: that this is
not the case and never has been.

    He has further instructed me to say that neither he nor the
Conservative Board of Finance is interested in your latest proposal.
In suggesting that Conservative policies and beliefs might be in some
way responsible for the few and regrettable lapses from the highest
standards of probity taking place recently in the City of London,
your series would be dangerously partial and ill-informed. In any
case it is not the policy of the Conservative Board of Finance to
fund purely commercial ventures.

    I am now returning your cheque in the sum of one thousand
pounds, drawn on the Bank of Guernsey, in favour of Brigadier Wyldbore-Smith.

Yours sincerely,

Brigadier L.H. Lee C.B.E.

Mr Henry Root
H.R.PRODUCTIONS
Suites 9-57
139 Elm Park Mansions
Park Walk
London, SW10   6th April 1987

Dear Mr Root,

Thank you for your letter of 5th April, enclosing your TV project
The WestEnders by Henry Root.

I think that with a certain amount of re-writing this could be a viable
product. I would say at once that the title strikes me as mistaken.
It suggests a parody, which the script seems not to be. The narrative
line - the story of two families whose fates become tragically inter-
locked under the shadow of corruption - is strong, though scarcely
original. To give it greater relevance today, I would suggest adding
a documentary dimension, perhaps interviewing on film some of the
protagonists in the scandals dealt with.

I am afraid that you seem to be mistaken in thinking that Sir David
Brown of Aston Martin is one of our directors and might be persuaded
to invest in your venture. Mr. Louis Brown, the night-club owner, was
a founding director of the company. Alas, he died quite recently.

We would be prepared, once the alterations I suggest have been effected,
to act as casting directors on your venture and to offer pre-production
advice.

Yours sincerely,

Clare Ogilvie

Clare Ogilvie.

139 Elm Park Mansions
Park Walk
London, SW10.

7th April 1987.

Ms Clare Ogilvie
Gordon & Ogilvie Ltd
22 Half Moon Street
London, W1

Dear Ms Ogilvie,

We are in receipt of your letter of 6th April. I note your information in the matter of Louis Brown (deceased), the night-club impresario, and suggest that for the convenience of punters in the future you mark him as deceased as such on your letter-heads or delete him.

Your suggestions re my script are of no interest to me. I note your availability to cast but would point out that I am myself experienced in the casting game having 'Spotlight' and assistance.

Yours sincerely,

Henry Root

Henry Root.

GORDON & OGILVIE LTD
22 Half Moon Street
London W1

Mr Joseph Columbo
Gambino, Ziskie, Columbo and Seltzer Inc
174 East 43rd Street
New York

7th April 1987

Dear Uncle Joe,

Guess what! I think I've come across that 'situation' you asked me to keep an eye out for.

A man called Henry Root wrote to the office the other day trying to raise money for some TV series he says he's written called 'The WestEnders'. He sounds a bit bonkers, Uncle Joe, and I would be surprised if the series ever happened - but that would be all the same to you, I imagine.

If you still want to 'lose' all that lovely money over here I'm sure this could be the answer. Anyway, his address is: 139 Elm Park Mansions, Park Walk, London, SW10. He really might be the mug you're looking for, I think.

My fondest love to Aunt Maria. I got a letter from her last week in which she said that you're beginning to get some feeling back in your legs and might be off the life-support system next year or the year after. That's brilliant news! What a silly business that was.

Ta ever so much for the Porsche. It's really great!

Your devoted niece,

Selina Sidey

Selina Sidey.

139 Elm Park Mansions
Park Walk
London, SW10.

7th April 1987.

Mr Graham Webster-Gardiner
Conservative Family Campaign
45 West Hill Avenue
Epsom
Surrey KT18 8JX.

Dear Webster-Gardiner,

Thank you for your unsolicited letter of 6th April enclosing literature re your excellent Conservative Family Campaign. I cert-ainly wish to join a club of which Dame Knight, Sir Braine and old Viscount Buckmaster are members, and I now return the enrollment form plus £10.

I agree with your exciting plans to tag and isolate homosexuals on the Isle of Wight, but might take issue with you re your slogan 'God is gracious and good'. I would myself prefer something a little more robust - 'God reads the Daily Telegraph', perhaps - at a time when we have all suffered enough from the activities of the gracious and good. God, surely, was never afraid to risk the bad opinion of do-gooders, visiting boils and thunder-bolts on liberals of the Guardian-reading sort - though Christ was a more convivial man from all accounts, a Spectator-reader at a guess, who always stood his round. Further I'd say that 'render unto Caesar' etc holds water as much now as it ever did.

That said, allow me to involve you in a scheme of mine. I enclose a copy of my latest TV series - THE WESTENDERS By HENRY ROOT - which, as you will see, traces the sad decline of this once great country from the so-called Sixties to the present day. Taking the form of a drama/documentary, it will contain filmed interviews with many of the sordid people caught up in the scandals of recent years (Lord Denning, Janie Jones, 'Jack' Profumo, Christine Keeler, Sir Saunders of Boots, Miss 'Fiona Wright', Cecil Parkinson and so forth.)

What do you think? Many leading Conservatives - Norman Tebbit, Edwina Currie, the Bishop of London, old Wyldebore-Smith - are four-square behind the enterprise, designating themselves as FRIENDS OF THE WESTENDERS by HENRY ROOT and proud to wear our T-Shirt. Would you or the CFC care to be advertised on my writing-paper as FRIENDS OF THE WESTENDERS by HENRY ROOT?

I look forward to hearing from you.

Let's tag some pansies!

Henry Root

Henry Root.

CONSERVATIVE FAMILY CAMPAIGN

Bringing the family back into focus

45 West Hill Avenue, Epsom, Surrey KT19 8JX. Tel: 03727 21027.   Messages to: 01 677 9775

Chairman: Graham Webster-Gardiner   Hon. Secretary: Antonia Hopkins   Consultant: Dr. Adrian Rogers MB BS

Mr Henry Root
139 Elm Park Mansions
Park Walk
LONDON SW10
14 April 1987

Dear Mr Root

Thank you for your letter of 7 April received 8 April. Thank
you in particular for deciding to become a member of CFC.
You should hear formally from our membership secretary,
Mrs Angela Gracey.

I am pleased that you agree with us about homosexuality. I
think the usage I made of the expression, "God is gracious and
good" referred particularly to the personal experience I had
gone through in 1986 when seriously ill and yet was wonderfully
ministered to by the Lord Jesus, and how He enabled CFC to
flourish during the period of my indisposition. There is no
question that God quite clearly pronounced judgement on those
who acted unrighteously, and this is clearly happening to those
who have abused themselves with drugs or used their bodies in
abnormal and unnatural ways as the homosexuals do.

Thank you for writing as you did.

Yours sincerely
CONSERVATIVE FAMILY CAMPAIGN

Graham Webster-Gardiner
Chairman

Professor Michael Zander
The Guardian
119 Farringdon Road
London, EC1.

Dear Professor Zander,

    I was surprised to read that my friend Harvey Proctor MP has been charged with gross indecency following the whacking of an art dealer in his Fulham Road apartment.

    Surely corporal punishment is widely encouraged by the present Government, and indeed my son Henry Jr was frequently whacked at Harrow School - not that it did him any good since he is now appearing in feathers on a pedestal at Paul Raymonde's 'La Vie En Rose'. You know a bit of law, I take it. Can I bring an action retrospectively against Harrow School for gross indecency?

    Further, at this time of Aids hysteria and so forth, does not corporal punishment at a distance, with or without the throwing of cream cakes, constitute safe sex?

    You'll be a busy man, I expect - as I am too, developing now THE WESTENDERS by HENRY ROOT - so I enclose a stamped addressed envelope for the convenience of your advice.

    Yours sincerely,

Henry Root

Henry Root.

---

12 WOODSIDE AVENUE.
LONDON. N.6.
TEL: 01-883 6257

May 25th 1987

Dear Mr Root,

    I must apologise for the inordinate delay in replying to your letter of April 9th. But as you rightly point out,I am a busy man. (My wife is also busy as is my son and my daughter - and her friend Jeremy,as you no doubt are yourself).

    I take your point about the value of beating. My only personal experience of the matter was as a schoolboy when I was beaten for eating six desserts. There was also the time a few years earlier when I was beaten at home for an offence committed by my brother. Both occasions remain happy memories.

    I doubt whether you will succeed in legal proceedings against Harrow School in respect of your son Henry Jr. but test cases of this kind are always enjoyable.

    I do not join you in Supporting the Iron Maiden at this time (though doubtless she would share your view about the value of beating)as 1987 is surely the Year of the Tactical Vote.

    Yours sincerely

Michael Zander

Michael Zander

Mr Henry Root
139 Elm Park Mans...
Lond...

CARLO GAMBINO
DANIEL ZISKIE
JOSEPH COLUMBO
AARON SELTZER

Mr Henry Root
139 Elm Park Mansions
Park Walk
London, SW10.

11th April 1987

Dear Mr. Root,

My niece Selina Sidey works for Gordon & Ogilvie, London Casting Agents.

She tells me you need finance for a TV product written by yourself. I presently have leisure resources available and the inclination at this time to expand my UK operation.

I intend to invest the sum of $2 million in your business in return for financial control. I will place certain associates of mine in London. They will run the operation day-to-day, reporting back to me.

You will, of course, accept this offer. You will find me a reasonable man.

Cordially yours,

Joe Columbo

Joseph Columbo.

---

139 Elm Park Mansions
Park Walk
London, SW10.

Mr Joseph Columbo
Gambino, Ziskie, Columbo & Seltzer Inc
174 East 43rd Street
New York.

15th April 1987.

Dear Columbo,
        Bog off.
        Yours sincerely,

Henry Root

Henry Root.

139 Elm Park Mansions
Park Walk
London, SW10.

Mr Joseph Columbo
Gambino, Ziskie, Columbo & Seltzer Inc
174 East 43rd Street
New York.

19th April 1987.

Dear Mr Columbo,

My mistake entirely. Your kind telephone call to this office
today made me realise how reasonable your offer was. I accept now
that I need your leisure expertise - financial and artistic (casting, wardrobe) - and I agree to all your terms.

There is ample room here for your associates - Smits, Ziskie,
Goldfarb, Seltzer, Eikenberry and Rachins - and I look forward to
their arrival in the UK on the 28th of this month in matching hats
and banjo cases (don't mind me, Joe - just my sense of humour!) I
will engage some turkeys here as you suggest - Picano, Mortimer,
McPeak - for the purposes of standing still in case the shit, as
you put it, hits the fan - allowing your people to return to the USA
untouched. I myself will, as you suggest, play a turkey too - under
the aliases Of Cox or Templeton, Development Editors.

I have had new writing paper printed as per your specifications
plus effected the changes in the script required by Ms Clare Ogilvie
of Ogilvie and Gordon Ltd and retitled it CRACK-UP by HENRY ROOT.
I will, of course, engage Gordon and Ogilvie Ltd as Casting Agents,
not least your niece, Selina.

It's all hands to the mattresses here!

Henry Root.

Henry Root.

139 Elm Park Mansions
Park Walk
London, SW10.

Ms Clare Ogilvie
Gordon & Ogilvie Ltd
22 Half Moon Street
London, W1.

19th April 1987.

Dear Ms Ogilvie,

It takes a large man to admit he was wrong, I think you'll
agree. The plain fact is I've had something of a re-think since
my letter to you of 7th April. I have decided to re-title my TV
series CRACK-UP by HENRY ROOT and to add a documentary dimension
(filmed interviews with many sordid participants in Sixties goings-
on and later - Parkinson, Lambton, Profumo etc) as per your sensible suggestions.

I enclose a full synopsis and cast breakdown and would now
like to appoint you as casting agents to the enterprise.

There is little point in employing a monkey and oneself
sitting on the organ in a comic hat, but here's one off the top
of the head: what about David Niven to play the part of Prime
Minister Macmillan as he then was?

Yours sincerely,

Henry Root.

Henry Root.

PS. I have decided, after careful thought, to accept some serious
venture capital plus leisure expertise from the USA (Gambino, Ziskie, Columbo & Seltzer Inc - Clean Towels and Pizzas). This will
necessitate a change of writing-paper with myself taking a lower
profile on the face of it. You will be seeing it shortly.

Telephone: 01-493 7632   Telegrams: Casting London

Henry Root Esq
139 Elm Park Mansions
Park Walk
London SW10   20th April 1987.

Dear Mr. Root,

Thank you for your letter of 19th of April with regard to your TV
development CRACK-UP. In fact you omitted to enclose the synopsis
and cast breakdown, but, ahead of receiving this, I can confirm
that we would be delighted to act as Casting Agents to the vehicle
at a weekly retainer of £250.

I will give you my initial casting suggestions as soon as I receive
the material on which to base them.

With regard to your suggestion that David Niven should play the part
of Prime Minister Macmillan, I have to remind you that he's dead.

Yours sincerely,

Clare Ogilvie

Clare Ogilvie.

Directors: Jane Gordon Clare Ogilvie Jacob Armanath Louis Brown

139 Elm Park Mansions
Park Walk
London, SW10.

21st April 1987.

Ms Clare Ogilvie
Gordon & Ogilvie Ltd
22 Half Moon Street
London, W1.

Dear Ms Ogilvie,
    I am well aware that Macmillan's dead, but he wasn't - was he? -
in 1963, the date of his scene in the series.
    Yours sincerely,

Henry Root.

Henry Root.

GORDON & OGILVIE LTD
22 Half Moon Street
London W1

Telephone: 01-493 7632

Telegrams: Casting London

Mr Henry Root
H.R.Productions
139 Elm Park Mansions
Park Walk
London, SW10.

22nd April 1987.

Dear Mr Root,

    Thank you for your letter of 21st April. I wasn't referring to Macmillan, but to David Niven. He, alas, is dead too.

    Yours sincerely,

Clare Ogilvie

Clare Ogilvie.

139 Elm Park Mansions
Park Walk
London, SW10.

23rd April 1987.

Ms Clare Ogilvie
Gordon & Ogilvie Ltd
22 Half Moon Street
London, SW10.

Dear Ms Ogilvie,

Niven dead? Dear God what next! The old story-teller gone,
an end to racontage re Flynn and Bogie, is that the size of it?
Surely it was that wise man John Mortimer who said of Niven: 'Our
meetings were all about laughter'? Still - mustn't brood. 'Our
and they go. The Moon's a Balloon. Chocks Away Gentlemen, Please.
Never liked him anyway.

Here's another: what about Milton Shulman to play the part of
my friend Lord Weidenfeld? Squat, fat-faced, foreign - not bad, eh?
One celebrity playing another or himself? There have been many precedents in this area of casting. Judge Welch of Senator McCarthy
fame went on to play himself, you may recall (or someone else - I
can't remember which) in many Hollywood films, not least 'Anatomy of
A Murder' with Jimmy Stewart.

What do you think?

Yours sincerely,

Henry Root.

Mr. Henry Root
H.R.Productions
139 Elm Park Mansions
Park Walk
London, SW10.

24th April 1987.

Dear Mr Root,

Thank you for your letter of 23rd April. Milton Shulman isn't
a judge.

Yours sincerely,

Clare Ogilvie

Clare Ogilvie.

---

139 Elm Park Mansions
Park Walk
London, SW10.

Ms Clare Ogilvie
Gordon & Ogilvie Ltd
22 Half Moon Street
London, W1.

25th April 1987.

Dear Ms Ogilvie,

I am well aware that Milton Shulman isn't a judge. Nor, however, is my friend Lord Weidenfeld. What have you got to say to
that?

Yours sincerely,

Henry Root

Henry Root.

GORDON & OGILVIE LTD
22 Half Moon Street
London W1

Mr Henry Root
H.R.Productions
139 Elm Park Mansions
Park Walk
London, SW10.

26th April 1987.

Dear Mr Root,

Thank you for your letter of 25th April. Lord Weidenfeld isn't a
judge, and Milton Shulman isn't a publisher.

Yours sincerely,

Clare Ogilvie.

---

139 Elm Park Mansions
Park Walk
London, SW10.

Ms Clare Ogilvie
Gordon & Ogilvie Ltd
22 Half Moon Street
London, W1.

27th April 1987.

Dear Ms Ogilvie,

Nor he is. Never mind. Probably can't act anyway.

What about Dirk Bogarde as Margaret, Duchess of Argyll? Once
saw him in a play on tour playing a window-box. Couldn't act, but
he looked good. Or was that Gladys Cooper?

Audacious but interesting, don't you think?

I now enclose the full synopsis of CRACK-UP, as promised, plus
cast breakdown.

Yours sincerely,

Henry Root.

CRACK-UP. A Television Series In Ten Episodes - by HENRY ROOT.

SYNOPSIS.

This timely and important series takes the form of a drama/
documentary tracing the sad decline of this once great country
over the past 25 years. It draws a connection between the
loosening of moral imperatives during the so-called Sixties
(Mary Quant, excreta down the chimney-pot, Roy Jenkins, the
Great Train Robbery, rocketing massage parlours - Dick West
saw it all, they say) and today's squalid scandals in the City
of London and in the Tory Party under Mrs Thatcher (Big Bangs,
Filofax, 'unusual payments').

A documentary element will be fed into the fictional story-line
by the deft inclusion of filmed interviews with many of the
disgusting people responsible for the scandals of the past two
decades - 'Jack' Profumo, Janie Jones, Sir Saunders of Boots,
Cynthia Payne, Jeremy Thorpe, Cecil Parkinson etc - folk who
thought they'd done their time in the wilderness but will now
find themselves back at square one in front of a peak-time
audience of millions.

The narrative element in the series is the tragic story of two
families - the Smallhamptons and the Dorsets. Norman Smallhampton
(50) - humble, industrious and honest - was born in the East End
and has worked his balls off in fish, providing for his wife,
Rita (48), and his two children, Kevin (22) and Tracey (18).
Kevin has repaid his father's industry by working hard himself,
obtaining fifteen 'A' levels and getting himself a job in the
overnight money house, Grenfell Morgan Carey Collier & Co plc.
The Dorsets, conversely - doomed, mad, privileged - have everything
that money and position can acquire except happiness and self-
respect. The family consists of the barmy Duke (66) and his spoilt
drunken wife, the Duchess (58), their son, the weak, pop-eyed
Marquis of Beauchamp (28) and their daughter, pretty, hopeless
Henrietta (21).

It happens, by ironic coincidence, that the Marquis of Beauchamp
and Kevin Smallhampton start work on the same day at Grenfell
Morgan Carey Collier & Co plc, where they immediately form a
dangerous friendship. In no time at all the evil Marquis
introduces young Smallhampton to hard drugs and sexual licence.
Discovering that his son has fallen in with a bad hat, a distraught
Smallhampton Sr starts his own investigation into City corruption,
in the course of which he breaks into the apartment of the
venomously beautiful Princess Soszynski, a self-employed Polish
woman, where he finds young Kevin taking drugs with Soszynski,
Beauchamp and their evil associates (bankers, bimbos, racial
stereotypes, brokers, gossip columnists, girls from the Thai
Embassy, Old Harrovians and so forth). Smallhampton lays about

him, boxing bankers and bimbos to the floor and dragging his son
to safety - but it is already too late. Kevin has become addicted
to the dreaded 'crack', and shortly thereafter he is arrested with
Soszynski, Beauchamp and their wicked associates in a front-page
bust.

With bulldog courage, Smallhampton Sr calls on the Duke of Dorset
at his stately seat in Wiltshire, inviting him to become Chairman
of Fathers Anonymous (FA), a vigilante group of fathers bent on
fighting the evils of drugs and money lust in Mrs Thatcher's
Britain. Alas, the distracted, half-mad Duke can scarcely follow
Smallhampton's arguments, so, realising that Dorset is a broken
man, Smallhampton leaves, determined to fight corruption on his
own. He forms FA and carries out a fearless investigation into
declining standards - 'You can run but you can't hide from Norman
Smallhampton' - interviewing many of the sordid protagonists in
the scandals of the past two decades (Lambton, Profumo, Parkinson).
He meets Max Hastings, Mary Whitehouse and Mrs Thatcher (praying
with the latter two against pornography in the toilet at No 10 -
a crucial scene); he is beaten up by Special Branch, drugged and
photographed with naked schoolboys by MI5 (and their City pay-
masters), but eventually he triumphs, cleaning up the City on his
own, closing down many banks and commodity houses and filling key
posts, such as Chairman of the Stock Exchange, with his own
nominees. He dances with the Duchess of Argyll; he has an affair
with Princess Michael of Kent; his story is published by Lord
Weidenfeld; he meets Geoffrey Wheatcroft. Finally, to the
applause of a grateful nation, he receives a long overdue peerage
from the Queen - which is all too late, alas, for his son Kevin,
who is 'cured' by a drug addiction centre practising the Minnesota
Method and is seen, in a final tragic episode, sitting alone in the
cold garden of a seaside clinic, mumbling distractedly to himself.
He didn't listen to his father. We're all guilty.

CAST BREAKDOWN.

PRINCIPALS.

NORMAN SMALLHAMPTON. 50. Burly, honest, indomitable. He has
punched his way up from the East End of London and now - through
the sweat of his brow - has money, high street leases and a ranch-
style duplex with lounge-diner at the right end of Acton Avenue.
It had been three-to-the-shirt where he was born and the outside
bucket, but now he plays tennis on Sundays with Ernie Wise and on
the fake grand piano in his executive lounge-diner there are signed
photographs of Lee Trevino, Lennie Bennett and Paul Raymonde. A
fighting bull of a man, he exemplifies the finest qualities of
'Englishness' from Henry VIII to Robert Maxwell.

RITA SMALLHAMPTON.   47. His wife. An ex-cocktail waitress, she now carries 36lbs of excess water and spends all her time reading kitchen equipment maintenance literature.

KEVIN SMALLHAMPTON.   21. Their son. Basically a good type, he is too easily led astray by the smart new friends he makes in the City and by the viciously beautiful Princess Soszynski.

TRACEY SMALLHAMPTON.   18. Their daughter. The apple of her father's eye, she has just won a place at Essex University where she is to study Sociology and Vitamins. Studious rather than pretty.

THE DUKE OF DORSET.   66. A dotty aristocrat, he keeps a pig on a lead and is quite ill-equipped to cope with the tragedy that now engulfs him.

THE DUCHESS OF DORSET.   57. His wife. Spoilt. Drunk. She is interested in nothing but her wardrobe of customised clothes.

THE MARQUIS OF BEAUCHAMP.   28. Their son and heir. Weak, decadent, jelly-jawed - if you look him in the eye he quivers like a defecating greyhound. One of the two villains of the piece, he corrupts anyone who hasn't already been corrupted by the vilely beautiful Princess Soszynski. (In an original draft, these two parts were written for James Fox and Dirk Bogarde, and Losey still echoes teasingly between the lines).

HENRIETTA.   21. Their daughter. Pretty, well-intentioned and confused, she never quite knows what to do - even when her brother, the pop-eyed Marquis, steals her jewellery to buy himself a fix.

PRINCESS SOSZYNSKI.   32. A self-employed Polish woman, a woman easily ignited in the early afternoon, she is as temptingly lush as a poisoned peach. A leather-clad sadist, she and her 'slave', the cherry-lipped Beauchamp, corrupt everyone with whom they come in contact.

SMALLER PARTS.

JOHN PROFUMO.   48 at the time of the action. An over-sexed politician, he wears monogrammed underwear and has a head like a racing tadpole. Later, he is to pay his debt to society.

MRS. PROFUMO. 'Jack' Profumo's fragrant wife. She stands by her husband in the glare of unwelcome publicity, posing with him in the East End and outside country churches.

STEPHEN WARD.   48. Society osteopath and international pervert. A victim of an historic injustice.

MERVYN GRIFFITH-JONES QC. Prosecuting counsel at the trial of
Stephen Ward ("Would you like this man to massage your wife or
servants?"). Bullying, ignorant and rude.

LORD DENNING. 82. In the Swinging Sixties he is up the creek
without a paddle. He is a butt for the excellent jokes of:

MANDY RICE-DAVIES. 22 at the time of the action. A celebrated
society wit, she has no difficulty in running rings round Lord
Denning.

LORD LAMBTON. 52. A sexual glutton.

NORMA LEVY. 36. A common callgirl and blackmailer.

NORMA LEVY'S PIMP. 32. He lives with his camera equipment on
top of Norma Levy's wardrobe.

CECIL PARKINSON. 54. Adulterer and political lightweight.

ANN PARKINSON. 51. She stands by her husband in the glare of
unwelcome publicity.

SARA KEAYS. 47. A bitter, unattractive single mother.

THE MAN IN THE MASK. A minister in Macmillan's government, at
cabinet meetings he is lowered from the ceiling on a kebab skewer
wearing high-heels and mail-order underwear.

JEFFREY ARCHER. 48. Ex-politician and airport author. He can
run a hundred yards in ten seconds and pays tarts to leave the
country. No one knows why.

MARY ARCHER. 44. His wife. A hard, boot-faced woman, she stands
by her husband in the glare of welcome publicity.

PETER RACHMAN. 60. Tory property developer.

RICHARD INGRAMS. 54. A pot-bellied Christian. Firm but fair,
stern but stupid, he is enlisted by Smallhampton in the fight
against corruption.

SIR RALPH HALPERN. 50. Over-sexed business tycoon. Chairman of
Boots. Attractive but ruthless.

FIONA WRIGHT. 22. One of Sir Halpern's many bimbos. Pretty but
common.

FRANCES EDMONDS. 40. A vulgar self-publicist.

ROBERT SAMPSON QC. 60. A distinguished, grey-haired barrister.
It is his unenviable task to defend the cherry-lipped Marquis of
Beauchamp.

SIR NICHOLAS GOODISON. 63. Money man and buff. One of the few
honourable men left in the City of London.

YOKO ONO. 54. She's been to hell and back.

ANNA RAEBURN. 40. She's looking more relaxed now that she's

discovered who she really is.

SIR PETER CAREY. 66. A hard nut. He is brought in by Smallhampton to clean up the Aegean stables that is Arthur Guiness plc.

JONATHAN ROSS. 22. A very private person. We're all guilty.

MARGARET, DUCHESS OF ARGYLL. 76. A self-made woman, she lives in
a hotel room surrounded by burly men and smart lawyers.

DUDLEY MOORE. 53. A pint-sized Romeo.

HENRY COOPER. 54. A gentle giant.

BILLY CONNOLLY. 46. Such is his insouciance that even his
constant references to 'big jobbies' scarcely give offence.

PAULA YATES. 30. Married to Billy Connolly. Author of 'Pop
Stars No 2s' (Virgin Books, £7.95).

VARIOUS OLD CODGERS who speak for common sense and reason. They
live in the real world and were not deceived by the so-called
Sixties. They smell like badgers and take their holidays in
Wales. They obtain sexual gratification by sitting suddenly
on the wrong end of their shooting-sticks. They are:

MAX HASTINGS. 50. A humourless Editor.

RICHARD WEST. 60. A prim old podge.

GEOFFREY WHEATCROFT. 48. A pouting columnist.

CHRISTOPHER BOOKER. 52. A comical social whatsit.

A.N. WILSON. 43. A prissy novelist.

BIT PARTS AND CAMEOS.

GREEK GEORGE. 34. A drug-dealer. A toad. Small. Fat. Evil.

ZAPHYRE. 52. Another drug dealer. Black. Cheerful. He laughs
a lot and carries the cocaine in his pork-pie hat.

EDWARD. 70. Judge Henry Herbert QC's clerk.

ARCHIBALD. 80. The half-mad Duke of Dorset's butler.

JUDGE HENRY HERBERT QC. 60. A kindly jurist, he is easily
persuaded not to bang up the disgusting Marquis of Beauchamp for
the ten years he so richly deserves.

PLUS:

Sleazebags, bimbos, racial stereotypes, leathery-skinned super-
bitches (Joan Collins, Stephanie Beacham, Vincent Price, etc),
the Great Train Robbers, the Kray Twins, Mary Quant, KGB agents,
gossip columnists, tarts, Tories, lesbians, girls from the Thai
Embassy, bankers, brokers, bonkers, bogglers, Sir Maurice Oldfield,
Sir Peter Wright, the Krankies, Milton Shulman, Old Harrovians,

CRACK-UP.   CAST BREAKDOWN (cont).

Nigel Dempster, junkies, fishy Christians, Old Bill, Lindy Benson,
Lord Astor, Jean Rook, Lord Stockton, Lord Hailsham, Mrs Thatcher,
Samantha Fox's mother.

& OGILVIE LTD
22 Half Moon Street
London W1

Mr Henry Root
139 Elm Park Mansions
Park Walk
London, SW10.

Dear Mr. Root,   28th April 1987.

Thank you for your letter of 27th April, enclosing at last the
synopsis of CRACK-UP and cast breakdown.

When is the expertise from America arriving?

I'm off on Monday for an extended holiday and may not be returning
for some time. In my absence you should address any further queries
to Selina Sidey of this office. You will find her very able and
most helpful.

Yours sincerely,

Clare Ogilvie

Clare Ogilvie.

---

                                      139 Elm Park Mansions
                                      Park Walk
                                      London, SW10.

Ms Selina Sidey
Gordon & Ogilvie Ltd   29th April 1987.
22 Half Moon Street
London, W1.

Dear Ms Sidey,

        Re CRACK-UP by HENRY ROOT, who's that old idiot? I want to
write to him.

        Yours sincerely,

Henry Root

Henry Root.

London...

32

Henry Root
lm And Television Copyrights
9 Elm Park Mansions
ark Walk
ondon, SW10.

30th April 1987.

Dear Mr Root,

Are you referring to Sir Laurens Van de Post?

Yours sincerely,

Selina Sidey

Selina Sidey.

FILM AND TELEVISION COPYRIGHTS

139 Elm Park Mansions
Park Walk
London SW10

Tel: 01 – 352 9689
Telegrams: Concept London

Ms Selina Sidey
Gordon & Ogilvie Ltd
22 Half Moon Street
London, W1.

1st May 1987.

Dear Ms Sidey,

That's the fellow. Well done. Knows Prince Charles, do you
see? My theory, re Prince Charles, is to blame his father, the Duke
of Edinburgh. Edinburgh gave Charles and Anne a pair of boxing
gloves apiece aged 8 and 6. The upshot? Anne knocked Charles spark
out, causing many of his later problems – levitating with Indians
in their underwear, sitting with fakirs on lighted gas-rings and
conversing with potted plants. Talking of which, what did your office
think of my idea re Dirk Bogarde playing Margaret, Duchess of Argyll?

And here's another: what about Jan Leeming as Sara Keays? Got
that air of steely vulnerability, don't you think, sickening but
effective with a certain sort of man. Once saw her sing 'Hullo Young
Lovers' on the Terry Wogan Show – Leeming, that is, not Keays. Don't
Know if Keays can sing – Leeming certainly couldn't.

Yours sincerely,

Henry Root

Henry Root.

PS.   My respects to your Uncle Joe when next you write to him.

FILM AND TELEVISION COPYRIGHTS

139 Elm Park Mansions
Park Walk
London SW10

Tel: 01 – 352 9689
Telegrams: Concept London

Sir Nicholas Goodison
Chairman of the Stock Exchange
The Stock Exchange
London EC2N 1HP.

4th May 1987.

Dear Sir Nicholas,

We're over here for some rumpy tumpy, to see some shows and to make a ten-part TV series which will blow the punters' socks off (synopsis enclosed).

As you will see, we're promoting the dodge as a full-frontal attack on declining standards in City toilets (cocaine-related brain seizures in the 'powder-room', right?), of a gentleman's word no longer being his bond - all that shit. Water off our backs, as off yours, I imagine, but to raise the mug capital and for the sake of dramatic so forth we are blaming the aforesaid skullduggery (crooks in pin-stripes, Tory MPs making multiple share applications under aliases - the biggest crap game in town - I don't have to tell you) on the so-called Sixties (Mary Quant, the Monkeys - remember them? - Roy Jenkins, the pill, Lady Chatterley, Grace Kelly - a Princess from the moment she was born, Sir Nicholas, yet speared between takes from behind by Coop and others in her mobile dressing-room - 'Dick' West saw it all, they say.)

Could we power-breakfast on this one? You make the play in this town, I'm told, and I play hard-ball myself. Over a kipper you could tell me your side of the story - post Big Bang you're taking a lot of flak, I hear. We intend to interview some doubtful types on film (Sir Johns Knott and Cuckney, les fils Dreyfus etc) and you may care to join them. Alternatively, being a busy man with many money-making engagements in the day, you might prefer simply to become a FRIEND OF CRACK-UP, as many moral leaders have already. (We will shortly be contacting Chief Constable Anderton, who recently bought a beard in a novelty shop and now claims to speak for God). I realise that you're not a moral leader, never claimed to be, in fact - sink the Belgrano, eh? That's the spirit! (or was that Sir Knott of Lazards?) - but it would nonetheless help us considerably were you to follow their example and wear our T-shirt. Post Big Bang it would reassure many mugs with their holiday money in stocks and bonds to know that you're against the bad hats after all.

Cordially yours,

Milt Goldfarb

Milton Goldfarb. Executive Producer.

Enc. CRACK-UP, Synopsis and Cast Breakdown.

CRACK-UP by HENRY ROOT.

Inter-Office Production Memo.

Date: 4th May 1987.

Time: 6pm.

ROOT to: Ziskie
Seltzer
Smits
Eikenberry
Rachins

Goldfarb's letter to Sir Nicholas Goodison to hand.

It's forceful - gamey, even - but a little too gamey, if I may
say so. The references to Coop and Monkeys might be confusing
to an Englishman, plus mention of Grace Kelly in this context
would be offensive to someone of Sir Goodison's age-group, within
which Princess Grace was much revered.

Not altogether Goldfarb's fault. It takes years of practice learning how to address these turkeys. Sir Goodison's a buff, knows
art and opera, do you see, not least al fresco, sweats off to
Glyndebourne in the afternoon with Levin, Lindy Benson, Wheatcroft
('Music's all the more agreeable, dear boy, for being heard in a
congenial setting, pass the saumon au paté' - that's what we're
up against when trying to pluck these mugs.)

I suggest that for the time being I address the punters as
per the enclosed to the Bishop of London and Judge Pickles QC,
which I append here as examples, either as myself, Root, or under
my noms de plumes of Templeton and Cox. Just until you pick up
our way of doing things, you understand.

Kindly tick to signify agreement.

FILM AND TELEVISION COPYRIGHTS

139 Elm Park Mansions
Park Walk
London SW10

Tel: 01 − 352 9689
Telegrams: Concept London

The Rt Rev Bishop of London
London House
8 Barton Street
London SW1P 3RX.

4th May 1987.

Your Grace,

I enclose a letter from the Pope. This refers to a ten-part TV drama/documentary which this company is developing in association with Gambino, Ziskie, Columbo & Seltzer (Clean Towels and Pizzas) of the USA. It will, we are confident, put back to square one many of the sordid people involved in the scandals of the past 25 years. And not before time, I think you will agree.

The series, entitled CRACK-UP by HENRY ROOT, will draw a connection between the loosening of moral imperatives during the so-called Sixties (Roy Jenkins, the Beatles, rocketing massage parlours and VD statistics - Christopher Booker foresaw it all, they say) and today's shenanigans in the City of London and in the Tory Party under Mrs Thatcher (Sir Saunders and his shredding-machine, brasserie types on the inside lane, teenagers in butcher-stripe shirts making multiple share applications under aliases - later to be defended by Alexander QC, himself a City watchdog).

Many of the squalid people involved in recent scandals - 'Jack' Profumo, Janie Jones, Lord Lambton, Buster Edwards, Cecil Parkinson and so forth - have already had the affrontery to agree to appear for us on film, and we are now canvassing leaders of the moral community - such as it is - asking them to give their support by designating themselves as FRIENDS OF CRACK-UP, prepared to wear our T-shirt.

I trust that you, who preside, after all, over the morals - such as they are - of our capital city, may be persuaded to do the same. It wouldn't do for the Church of England to lag behind the Pope in this respect.

Let's stuff the Tories!

Yours sincerely,

Henry Root

Henry Root.

Enc.   Letter from the Pope, dated 23rd April 1987.

SECRETARIAT OF STATE

No. 31688/A

FROM THE VATICAN, **23rd April 1987**

Dear Mr Root,

     The Holy Father has asked me to thank you for your letter of 25th March. He wishes you well with CRACK UP, which he believes to be a worthwhile undertaking. He cannot do as you request on behalf of Derby County - but he wishes them well too.

     With the Holy Father's blessings.

Monsignor G.B. Re

Assessor

Henry Root, Esq.,
139 Elm Park Mansions,
Park Walk,
London, S.W.10

8th June 1987

Dear Mr. Root,

Thank you for asking me to be a friend of Crack-up. As you have heard from my secretary, my delay in replying is due to the fact that I have been in Canada and the U.S.A. for theological conferences and not, as you assumed, to neglect or discourtesy on my part.

I agree that attention needs to be drawn to the extent of the moral decline in this country over the past twenty-five years, but if such action is to lead to an improvement, which I assume is your purpose, I think three points need to be borne in mind.

First, the question must be asked, "Why did the process begin in the Sixties?" I do not believe that such major shifts in public attitudes arise spontaneously like mutations. No one has yet really tried to answer that question. I would suggest that the fundamental cause can be traced back to the Age of the Enlightenment in the Eighteen Century, the profound effects of which are being recognized today in many disciplines as well as in the moral sphere. Perhaps the most important change was the rejection of obedience on the grounds that it violated human dignity. Feverbach, for example, recognized that belief in God requires obedience and for this reason, rejected belief in God. Why these effects suddenly acquired particular force in the Sixties is a matter for debate, but I suspect that one reason was that because of developments in technology, medicine and social provision, people no longer had to face the consequences of their actions to the same extent.   The impact of A.I.D.S. has re-introduced the relationship between cause and effect in behaviour.

Secondly, it is often assumed wrongly that principle and compassion are incompatible, whereas true compassion is only possible on the basis of principle.   A doctor can only begin to heal because he knows what a healthy human being is and works from and towards that ideal.   He will not heal if he merely acquiesces in a person's diseased state.   In the moral sphere, forgiveness does not mean condonation.   On the contrary forgiveness is only possible when sin is recognized.

Thirdly, I believe that those of us who have some public responsibility in the moral sphere must seek to be positive in our response to the moral decline and not merely negative.   It was for this reason that when recently I was asked to speak at the National Convention of Mrs. Whitehouse's organization, N.V.A.L.A., I spoke on 'The Splendour of Chastity' as I did also in Los Angeles in May.

I believe that one of the most important needs today is the recovery of the sense of responsibility which true freedom requires, rather than the seeking of excuses which enables us to evade it or put the responsibility on to others.

Trying to act responsibly myself, I should be grateful for your comments on what I have said, before saying whether I am willing to be numbered among the Friends of Crack-up.

Yours sincerely,

+ Graham London:

FILM AND TELEVISION COPYRIGHTS

139 Elm Park Mansions
Park Walk
London SW10

Tel: 01 – 352 9689
Telegrams: Concept London

1st May 1987.

Judge James Pickles QC
Sheffield Crown Court
Sheffield S1 1EH.

Dear Judge Pickles,

I watched your appearance on last week's 'Terry Wogan Show'
with interest. You have a good head and spoke with resonance, though
a touch of humour might not have come amiss. Between anecdotes at
Hogg's expense you expressed regret at not having opted at a younger
age for a career in vaudeville. This being so, I have an offer which
might appeal. In association with Gambino, Ziskie, Columbo & Seltzer
Inc of the USA, we are developing here a ten-part TV series which
will trace many of our present ills (Boy George, Sir Saunders, condom
advertisements on BBC2) back to the scandals of the so-called Sixties
(the Great Train Robbery, the Carolines Charles and Coon).

One of the more recent scandals in which we have acquired
exclusive worldwide rights is the so-called 'Marquis of Beauchamp
affair' and we will be filming a scene in which the poor distracted
youth received greater compassion from your colleague Judge Henry
Herbert QC than many thought he deserved. Beauchamp himself is to
be played by Anthony Andrews of Brideshead notoriety and his father,
the barmy Duke of Dorset, into whose arms the half-witted youth fell
sobbing after the verdict, by Lord Laurence of Olivier. We have
recently decided that it would add greatly to the authority of the
scene were the part of Judge Herbert to be played by a 'professional'.

Would you care to take the role? I would remind you that there
have been many binding precedents in this area. To cite but one:
Judge Welch of Senator McCarthy fame later appeared as himself with
some skill and to his own advantage in many films not least 'Anatomy
of A Murder' with James Stewart, Lee Remick and Ben Gazzara (whatev
happened to him, I wonder?)

I look forward to hearing from you.

Yours sincerely,

Jeremy Cox

Jeremy Cox. Development Editor.

FILM AND TELEVISION COPYRIGHTS

139 Elm Park Mansions
Park Walk
London SW10

Tel: 01 – 352 9689
Telegrams: Concept London

Ms Selina Sidey
Gordon & Ogilvie Ltd
22 Half Moon Street
London W1.

7th May 1987.

Dear Selina,

    I have been appointed to do the casting on CRACK-UP at this end and to liase with you. It would be nice to have lunch some time.

    Mr Root wonders whether Jean Rook could play herself. What do you think?

    Yours,

Julia Mortimer

Julia Mortimer.

GORDON & OGILVIE LTD
22 Half Moon Street
London W1

Telephone: 01-493 7632

Telegrams: Casting London

Ms Julia Mortimer
Film And Television Copyrights
139 Elm Park Mansions
Park Walk
London, SW10.

8th May 1987.

Dear Julia,

Golly - I very much doubt it! She's <u>far</u> too common surely? I
expect she's mad keen to get on television, however - even as
herself - so why don't you write to her, asking for a recent
photograph? I suppose she could always play Margaret, Duchess of
Argyll - should Dirk Bogarde turn us down.

Lunch would be brilliant. Give me a ring soonest and we'll fix
something up.

Yours,

Selina Sidey.

Directors: Jane Gordon Clare Ogilvie Jacob Armanath Louis Brown

Jimmy Smits Milton G

FILM AND TELEVISION COPYRIGHTS

Ms Jean Rook
The Daily Express
Fleet Street
London EC4.

139 Elm Park Mansions
Park Walk
London SW10

Tel: 01 – 352 9689
Telegrams: Concept London

10th May 1987.

Dear Ms Rook,

As you may have heard, this company is developing a TV drama/documentary called CRACK-UP, which will take the lid off recent scandals and feature many celebrities. Do you think you could play yourself? If you do, could you possibly send me your best recent photograph?

Thank you so much.

Yours sincerely,

Julia Mortimer

Julia Mortimer. Casting Director.

DAILY EXPRESS

Express
Newspapers
p.l.c.

121 Fleet Street
London EC4P 4JT
Telephone
01-353 8000
Telex No. 21841
Cable Address
Express London

13 May 1987

Ms Julia Mortimer
139 Elm Park Mansions
Park Walk
LONDON
SW10

Dear Ms Mortimer

Thank you for your letter and how very kind of you to ask me
for the photograph, which I am very happy to send to you.

Yours sincerely

Jean Rook
Assistant Editor

Best wishes
Jean Rook

48. Registered office: 121 Fleet Street, London EC4P 4JT

Ref. SPP2

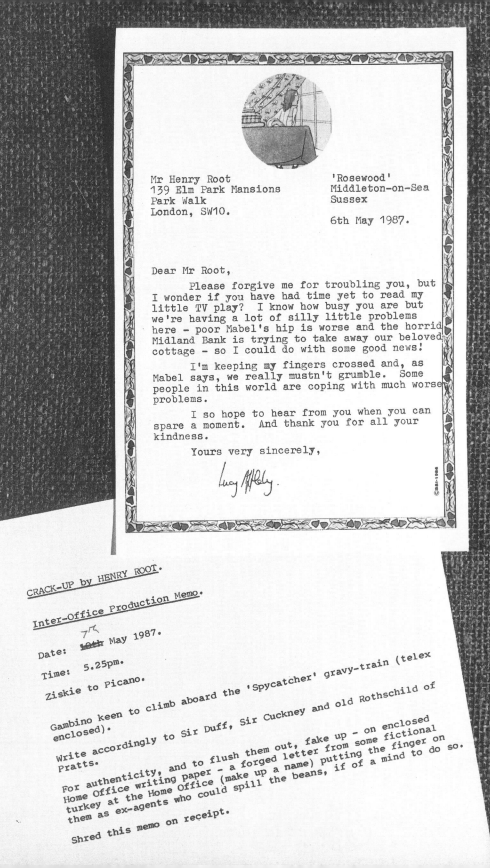

Mr Henry Root
139 Elm Park Mansions
Park Walk
London, SW10.

'Rosewood'
Middleton-on-Sea
Sussex

6th May 1987.

Dear Mr Root,

    Please forgive me for troubling you, but I wonder if you have had time yet to read my little TV play? I know how busy you are but we're having a lot of silly little problems here – poor Mabel's hip is worse and the horrid Midland Bank is trying to take away our beloved cottage – so I could do with some good news!

    I'm keeping my fingers crossed and, as Mabel says, we really mustn't grumble. Some people in this world are coping with much worse problems.

    I so hope to hear from you when you can spare a moment. And thank you for all your kindness.

    Yours very sincerely,

Lucy Appleby.

CRACK-UP by HENRY ROOT.

Inter-Office Production Memo.

Date: ~~10th~~ 7th May 1987.

Time: 5.25pm.

Ziskie to Picano.

Gambino keen to climb aboard the 'Spycatcher' gravy-train (telex enclosed).

Write accordingly to Sir Duff, Sir Cuckney and old Rothschild of Pratts.

For authenticity, and to flush them out, fake up – on enclosed Home Office writing paper – a forged letter from some fictional turkey at the Home Office (make up a name) putting the finger on them as ex-agents who could spill the beans, if of a mind to do so.

Shred this memo on receipt.

FILM AND TELEVISION COPYRIGHTS

139 Elm Park Mansions
Park Walk
London SW10

Tel: 01 – 352 9689
Telegrams: Concept London

Sir Anthony Duff
Head of MI5
c/o The National Westminster Bank
17 The Hard
Portsea
Hampshire.

8th May 1987.

Dear Sir Anthony,

Mr Nicholas Coldstream of the Home Office informs us that you are 'a man with a finger in many pies'.

The background to the correspondence is that this company, together with Gambino, Ziskie, Columbo & Seltzer Inc of the USA, is currently developing a ten-part TV series by myself – CRACK-UP by HENRY ROOT – which will trace the moral collapse of this once great country over the past 25 years.

The muddy field of espionage (leaks, disinformation, moles, betrayals, the head of MI6 dancing with rent boys above the Markham Arms, that old fraud Wright with corks on his hat) is one, of course, in which we'll want to turn over a few old sods, so we wrote recently to the Home Office seeking the names of those who might be prepared to spill the beans on camera. Today we received the enclosed reply from Coldstream nominating yourself, Sir John Cuckney of Westland Helicopters and Lord Rothschild of the bank as ex-spies who could help us.

Would you care to be interviewed on film, reassuring the public that the espionage arm of this once great country has been 'cleaned up' under your command? We could meet at your convenience within a few days notice – with or without camera crew, continuity and grip – either at the 'cover address' of your Hampshire bank or at your Curzon Street headquarters. Perhaps you could let me know a suitable date for yourself.

Yours sincerely,

Henry Root.

Henry Root.

Enc.   Letter, dated 27th April, from Mr Nicholas Coldstream of the Home Office to Miss Picano, Script Editor, CRACK-UP.

Robins Daniel Ziskie Aaron Seltzer Sandy McPeak Jill Eikenberry Jeremy Co
Max Templeton Julia Mortimer

HOME OFFICE
Queen Anne's Gate London SW1H 9AT

Direct line 01-213 3127
Switchboard 01-213 3000

Your reference

Our reference AT 467

Date 27th April 1987

<u>PRIVATE AND CONFIDENTIAL</u>

Dear Ms Picano,

Thank you for your letter of 20th April 1987. The Home Secretary has asked me to say that while he thoroughly endorses the idea of CRACK-UP he cannot be seen in public to be in any way involved with the programme, worthy though its aims undoubtedly are. For this reason he feels that he cannot accept your invitation to become a FRIEND OF CRACK-UP.

With regard to this country's appalling security record, he suggests that you write - enclosing a synopsis of your series - to the following: Sir Anthony Duff, presently the head of MI5, Sir John Cuckney, the Chairman of Westland Helicopters and Lord Rothschild, who has a finger in many pies. All three gentlemen could be of great assistanc to you were they prepared to say what they know.

The Home Secretary wishes you every success with the project.

Yours sincerely,

Nicholas Coldstream.

Ms Angela Picano
Script Editor
H.R. Productions
139 Elm Park Mansions
Park Walk
London, SW10.

FILM AND TELEVISION COPYRIGHTS

139 Elm Park Mansions
Park Walk
London SW10

Tel: 01 – 352 9689
Telegrams: Concept London

Lord Lane
The Lord Chief Justice
The Royal Courts of Justice
The Strand
London WC2.

10th May 1987.

Dear Lord Lane,

I congratulate you on the speech you made in Bristol recently in which you spoke up against declining standards. That's our game too. As you may have already heard, we are currently developing a ten-part TV series entitled CRACK-UP by HENRY ROOT which will trace the moral collapse of this country from Mary Quant to Jeffrey Archer.

I won't confuse you with production details - suffice it to say that we are negotiating with Judge James Pickles QC to play the part in our series of Judge Henry Herbert QC, who, as you will remember, presided at the trial of the pop-eyed Marquis of Beauchamp, ostentatiously failing to send the miserable youth to the pokey for the ten years he so richly deserved.

I know what you're thinking. You're thinking: 'What marquee value is there in the name of Pickles? You can't bank Pickles. These guys must have just stepped off the out-of-town bus, their trousers held up by string.' Not so, your lordship. We know what we're doing. We're going for maximum authenticity here. We do have a problem, though. Since engaging Pickles to appear as Herbert, I have had some doubts. Is it compatible with the dignity of the court for a working judge to appear in make-up in our lounge-rooms as another judge? Pickles himself has no doubts at all, but he's an impetuous man, as you probably know, and I can't help wondering whether you and I don't have a responsibility, both to the court and to Pickles, to save Pickles from himself. What's your ruling?

Would you like meanwhile to become a FRIEND OF CRACK-UP as many spokemen for traditional standards and responsible TV - Mary Whitehouse, the Bishop of London, the Archbishop of York etc - already have. I'm not suggesting that supporting CRACK-UP is the only Christ-thing to do, but failing to do so does look fishy.

It's not my habit to inconvenience such a busy man, so I now enclose a fiver either for yourself or for the charity of your choice.

Let's give some villains some extra porridge!

Yours sincerely,

Max Templeton

Max Templeton. Executive Producer.

12 May 1987

Dear Mr Templeton,

Thank you for your letter of 10 May.

I note your suggestion that I should become a "Friend of Crack-up". I am grateful to you for the suggestion but I do not think that it would be proper for me to accept it.

So far as Judge Pickles is concerned, I am sure that your wisdom will dictate the right course for you to take.

I hope that you will not think me ungracious, but it would not be proper for me to accept the money which you so generously sent me even as a donation to the charity of my choice.

I return the £5 herewith.

I appreciate the fact of your writing to me.

Yours sincerely

Geoffrey Lane

Max Templeton Esq
Executive Producer
H R Productions
Suites 9-57, 139 Elm Park Mansions,
Park Walk,
LONDON SW10

Encls: £5.

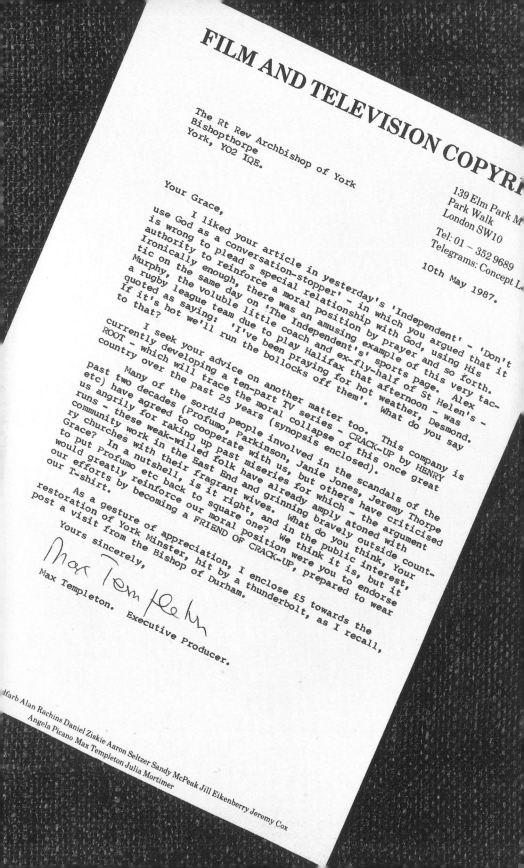

FILM AND TELEVISION COPYRI

139 Elm Park M
Park Walk
London SW10

Tel: 01 – 352 9689
Telegrams: Concept L

10th May 1987.

The Rt Rev Archbishop of York
Bishopthorpe
York, YO2 1QE.

Your Grace,

I liked your article in yesterday's 'Independent' - 'Don't use God as a conversation-stopper' - in which you argued that it is wrong to plead s special relationship with God, using His authority to reinforce a moral position by prayer and so forth. Ironically enough, there was an amusing example of this very tactic on the same day on 'The Independent's' sports page. Alex Murphy, the voluble little coach and ex-fly-half of St Helen's - a rugby league team due to play Halifax that afternoon - was quoted as saying: 'I've been praying for hot weather, Desmond. If it's hot we'll run the bollocks off them'. What do you say to that?

I seek your advice on another matter too. This company is currently developing a ten-part TV series - CRACK-UP by HENRY ROOT - which will trace the moral collapse of this once great country over the past 25 years (synopsis enclosed).

Many of the sordid people involved in the scandals of the past two decades (Profumo, Parkinson, Janie Jones, Jeremy Thorpe etc) have agreed to cooperate with us, but others have criticised us angrily for raking up past miseries for which - the argument runs - these weak-willed folk have already amply atoned with community work in the East End and grinning bravely outside counttry churches with their fragrant wives. What do you think, Your Grace? In a nutshell, is it right, and in the public interest, to put Profumo etc back to square one? We think it is, but it would greatly reinforce our moral position were you to endorse our efforts by becoming a FRIEND OF CRACK-UP, prepared to wear our T-shirt.

As a gesture of appreciation, I enclose £5 towards the restoration of York Minster, hit by a thunderbolt, as I recall, post a visit from the Bishop of Durham.

Yours sincerely,

Max Templeton.

Max Templeton. Executive Producer.

York (0904) 707021

BISHOPTHORPE
YORK
YO2 1QE

13 May 1987

Dear Mr Templeton,

Thank you for your letter about my article in the <u>Independent</u>. I am glad you found it helpful.

I am afraid a great deal of prayer takes the form of the prayer ascribed to Alex Murphy, but I would not want to be too hard on it because I suspect that those who use it do not seriously believe that it works!

As regards your proposed T.V. series, I can see the value in charting moral decline over the past 25 years, but I hope this might be balanced by the recognition that in some respects we are also a kinder, less judgemental society, learning rather painfully how to cope with moral and cultural pluralism.

I/too that you will avoid the most obvious targets. The /hope trouble with raking up old scandals is not simply that you may hurt the people concerned, who may perhaps already have been hurt enough, but that you will give the impression that certain people and certain sins can somehow be held to account for the moral decline you are attempting to chart.

I would myself be much more interested in analysis of the changing assumptions underlying say T.V. soap opera and comedy shows. Or you could analyse the subtle distortions in the popular press through headlines designed to appeal to people's prejudices. You might also analyse, not the well known city scandals, but the changes in normal assumptions about what is acceptable behaviour in the business world and what sort of rewards in terms of money perks etc. top business people now expect. You could look at the decline of moral conviction in the university world and the contraction of moral vision in once great organisations like the trades unions.

These to my mind are far more important indicators of what has been happening in our society than silly stories about Profumo and Jeremy Thorpe.

I fear these comments will not be of much help to you, but at least they indicate a different standpoint from that of Mr Anderton and Mrs Whitehouse.

Thank you for the £5 which I will pass on to the Minster Fund.

Yours sincerely,

John Ebor:

Max Templeton Esq
H.R. Productions
Suites 9-57, 139 Elm Park Mansions
Park Walk
LONDON SW10

FILM AND TELEVISION COPYRIGHTS

139 Elm Park Mansions
Park Walk
London SW10

Tel: 01 – 352 9689
Telegrams: Concept London

Sir Kit McMahon
Chairman
The Midland Bank plc
Poultry
London, EC2P 2BX.

10th May 1987.

Dear Sir Kit,

This is a concert party, over here from New York to wing a couple of mug punters, see some girls in their underwear and make a ten-part TV series. Further, I am persuaded by the positive PR attendant upon your recent appointment and your company's ballsy new advertising campaign ('We back business. We don't hold business back!') to switch our various accounts from Lloyds plc – Rumpole of the Baily and the horse inspire little confidence, I find – to your good selves. Before I do, however, perhaps you could reassure me on one point. I have read in the papers recently that City banks, as a consequence of the hard drugs epidemic among whizz kids post Sir Goodison's Big Bang, are now reporting directly to the police all banking movements in excess of $9,000,000. I frequently switch monies in excess of this to Bogota and back, so I would like your assurance that the remittance to you of my first substantial dollar draft would not be accompanied by a visit to our HQ of Drugs Squad officers tipped off by you. Could create the wrong impression. Imagine this: we're casting the ingenue ('Would you like to try for better billing, dear?') or plucking a 48-hour Jap and – BANG! – six busies in tall hats come head-first through our front-door snatching dangerous drugs out of thin air like French conjurors producing doves from nowhere. Don't tell me, Sir Kit – I know your old Bill's attitude to evidence.

Concerning the TV series: entitled CRACK-UP, it's hot and timely, tracing the moral collapse of your country from the Sixties to the present day. I'm a money man like you, so I won't confuse you with artistic matters (if you wish, I'll get one of our Script Editors – Templeton, Cox, Picano etc – to forward you a synopsis under separate cover). I'll come straight to the point. We're looking for development money to cover what we in the business call 'above the line costs' (script, breakfasts, location research – the George V Paris, Bogota and so forth) in the sum of £100,000. I won't blind you with science: suffice it to say that the total budget is £10 million and the development money will carry 1% of the net profits (we're talking points here) unless revolving in our next production (some punters prefer a roll-over arrangement, we find) plus residuals (Australia, what have you, together with repeats and merchandising).

Don't flash this all over the City. Perhaps we could make an appointment to meet, or, should you first want fuller details, I could bike you round an itemised budget.

Cordially,

Milton Goldfarb. Finance Director.

GAMBINO, ZISKIE, COLUMBO & SELTZER INC.
CLEAN TOWELS & PIZZAS

174 East 43rd Street, New York, N.Y. 10022. Tel: 212-873-4833

CARLO GAMBINO
DANIEL ZISKIE
JOSEPH COLUMBO
AARON SELTZER

Mr Daniel Ziskie
Film and Television Copyrights
139 Elm Park Mansions
Park Walk
London, SW10.

15th May 1987

Dear Daniel,

Goldfarb's letter to Sir McMahon to hand. Root was right. He's a loose cannon,
Dan. Dispose of him.

Regards,

Joe

Joseph Columbo

J. Gurnett Personal Management Limi

MANAGING DIRECTOR:
J. L. GURNETT

2 NEW KINGS
LONDON SW6
Telephone: 01-736
Facisimile: 01-736

Jeremy Cox, Esq.,
Development Editor,
H.R. Productions,
Suites 9 - 57,
139 Elm Park Mansions,
Park Walk
London S.W.10.

13th May 1987.

Dear Mr. Cox,

Thank you for your letter of 1st May sent to my client
Judge James Pickles.

Before we could indicate Judge Pickles' interest in your
proposal we would, of course, have to see the synopsis
of the scene you refer to, plus an outline of the series.

Also, which TV channel has commissioned you to develop the
series - is it for the U.K. or overseas. Would it be a weekly
series and for how many weeks. The proposed dates for shooting
and the location of same.

If you could let me have all the above information Judge Pickles
would then consider same and I would get back to you in due course
regarding fees etc.

Also, have you definitely contracted Lord Oliver and Anthony Andrews
for the series and the names of other people in the cast.

I look forward to hearing from you.

Yours sincerely,

Jo Gurnett

Jo Gurnett

J. Gurnett Personal Management Limited

MANAGING DIRECTOR:
J. L. GURNETT

CLIENT LIST – MARCH 1987

2 NEW KINGS ROAD
LONDON SW6 4SA
Telephone: 01-736 7828
Facsimile: 01-736 5455

TONY BAKER

TONY BLACKBURN — Presenter BBC TV "No Limits"

WILLIAM BOYDE — BBC Radio London

KEN BRUCE — "East Enders" – James Willmott-Brown

GLYNN CHRISTIAN — BBC Radio Two

GRAHAM DENE — BBC TV Breakfast Time Food Adviser. BBC Radio 2 Gloria Hunniford Show, Author.

JOHN DUNN — Capital Radio Weekdays 11.00 a.m.

GREG EDWARDS — BBC Radio 2. Weekdays 5.00 p.m.

KENNY EVERETT — Capital Radio Tuesdays/Fridays 8.00 p.m. Saturdays 5.00 p.m.

ANNA FORD — BBC TV Own Series. Capital Radio Saturdays 11.00 a.m.

PAUL HEINEY — Numerous TV and Radio Appearances.

GLORIA HUNNIFORD — BBC TV "In At the Deep End, "Travel Show" etc. BBC Radio 4.

CARON KEATING — BBC Radio 2 Weekdays 2.30 p.m. LWT "Sunday Sunday", "Newly Wed Game" etc.

RODDY LLEWELLYN — Presenter BBC TV "Blue Peter"

~~DIANA MORAN~~ — Gardening adviser BBC TV & Radio

~~Green Goddess BBC TV. Health and fitness and beauty expert.~~

ROBERT KILROY-SILK — BBC TV "Day To Day" Weekdays 9.05 a.m.

JEFF THACKER — Choreographer/Director. Numerous TV & Stage Shows, Pantos etc.

TOMMY VANCE — BBC Radio 1. Friday Rock Show.

ROBBIE VINCENT — BBC Radio London. BBC TV "Hospital Watch"

DAVID WIGG — Music Writer "Daily Express". Interviewer Channel 4 "Mirror Image"

TERRY WOGAN — BBC TV

STEVE WRIGHT — BBC Radio 1 Weekdays 3.00 p.m. BBC TV "Top of the Pops"

Licensed in accordance with the Employment Agencies Act 1973 No. SE 5509
VAT Registration No. 245 3447 63 Company Registration No. 1383908 Registered Offices 16/18 New Bridge Street, EC4.
Any offer contained in this letter does not constitute a contract.

FILM AND TELEVISION COPYRIGHTS

139 Elm Park Mansions
Park Walk
London SW10

Tel: 01 – 352 9689
Telegrams: Concept London

Jo Gurnett Esq
J. Gurnett Personal Management Ltd
2 New King's Road
London, SW6.

18th May 1987.

Dear Jo,

Your letter of 13th May re Judge Pickles to hand. We are delighted by Pickles's initial positive response to our proposal and now
enclose a scene from CRACK-UP in which your client would play the
part of Judge Henry Herbert QC. I must point out that we would, of
course, want Judge Pickles to be screen-tested before a definite
offer could be made.

With regard to your queries: is it for the UK or overseas? you
ask. The answer is yes. Lord Olivier, alas, has been compelled to
withdraw from shooting for reasons of health but we are in active
negotiation with Sir John Gielgud's agents with regard to his taking
over the small part of the barmy Duke of Dorset. There is no problem
with Anthony Andrews for the part of the half-witted Marquis of
Beauchamp.

Thank you for sending me a copy of your client list and other
valuable suggestions. I can't say I've ever cared much for the work
of Robert Kilroy-Silk, but well done for trying!

I look forward to hearing from you when Pickles has read the
script.

Yours sincerely,

Jeremy Cox. Development Editor.

Enc: CRACK-UP, Episode 8, scene 3.

Jimmy Smits ~~Milton Goldfarb~~ Alan Rachins Daniel Ziskie Aaron Seltzer Sandy McPeak Jill Eikenberry Jeremy Cox
Angela Picano Max Templeton Julia Mortimer

CRACK-UP. Episode 8. Scene 2. INTERIOR. JUDGE HENRY HERBERT QC'S room at Knightsbridge Crown Court. JUDGE HERBERT QC, a distinguished silver-haired man in his late fifties or early sixties, is reading some papers at his desk. There is a knock on the door.

JUDGE HERBERT QC: Come!

(Enter his clerk, EDWARD).

EDWARD: You have some visitors, your Honour.

JUDGE HERBERT QC (glancing at his watch): At this hour? Who can they be?

EDWARD: Mr Robert Sampson QC, your Honour, who is defending that disgusting young man the Marquis of Beauchamp, and his father, the half-mad Duke of Dorset.

RICHARD WEST: The real madmen, of course, are not the patients in top security hospitals but the psychiatrists who let them loose to kill again.

PEREGRINE WORSTHORNE: I wish I could believe that the long-term Broadmoor prisoner would be _less_ of a danger to the general public rather than more as a result of studying sociology at the Open University.

JUDGE HERBERT QC: Thank you, Edward. Show them in.

FADE.

CONSERVATIVE FAMILY CAMPAIGN

Bringing the family back into focus

45 West Hill Avenue, Epsom, Surrey KT19 8JX. Tel: 03727 21027.

Hon. Secretary: Antonia Hopkins

Chairman: Graham Webster-Gardiner

Messages to: 01 677 9775

Consultant: Dr. Adrian Rogers MB BS

// May 1987

Dear Friend,

GENERAL ELECTION 1987

We need the help of every single one of you in the next few weeks.

Firstly, we should all pray for the return of Mrs. Margaret Thatcher as our Prime Minister with a renewed Mandate for the Conservative Government. In particular we should pray for the destruction of the Labour Party which is increasingly an agent for the promotion of homosexuality, feminism, and other anti-Christian attitudes and policies. I ask you not only to pray as individuals but to ask prayer groups and churches with which you are associated to join in using this most vital of all the weapons at our disposal. Especially I ask you to pray for each of the individual candidates who are members of the Conservative Family Campaign, who will be seeking election to the House of Commons.

Secondly, we need your practical assistance to ensure the return of all our existing Conservative Family Campaign Members of Parliament and the election of prospective Parliamentary Candidates who have joined CFC. The practical assistance normally required of each of these would be the distribution of literature and canvassing voters in their respective constituencies. Any amount of help, however brief, is most definitely of value; but those who feel able to go and spend more than one day in a particular constituency can nearly always be found accommodation in a friendly home.

For your information members of Conservative Family Campaign that we request you actively support are as follows:

CANDIDATE	CONSTITUENCY	MAJORITY	PERCENTAGE MAJORITY
Michael Bates	Tynebridge	11,693 (Lab.)	31.3 %
David Sparrow	Manchester Wythenshawe	10,684 (Lab.)	25.2 %
Graham Webster-Gardiner	Newport E Gwent	2,630 (Lab.)	6.5 %

/ i...

SPONSORS: Mr. David Amess M.P., The Rt. Hon. Sir Bernard Braine DL M.P., Mr. Peter Bruinvels M.P., The Viscount Buckmaster O.B.E., F.R.G.S., Mr. William Cash M.P., Sir Fred Catherwood M.E.P., Lady Colman J.P., Rev. Peter Dawson O.B.E., Mr. Den Dover M.P., Mr. Harry Greenway M.P., Mr. Peter Griffiths M.P., Mr. Ken Hargreaves M.P., Dame Jill Knight O.B.E. M.P., Sir Hugh Rossi M.P., Mr. Ivor Stanbrook M.P., Mr. T.E. Utley ...

CANDIDATE	CONSTITUENCY	MAJORITY	PERCENTAGE MAJORITY
Ken Hargreaves	Hyndburn	21(Con.)	0 %
Peter Bruinvels	Leicester E	933(Con.)	1.9 %
David Amess	Basilden	1,379(Con.)	3.1 %
Sir Hugh Rossi	Hornsey and Wood Green	3,899(Con.)	7.4 %
Harry Greenway	Ealing N		
Mrs. Ann Winterton	Congleton	6,291(Con.)	12.3 %
Den Dover	Chorley	8,459(Con.)	17.2 %
Ivor Stanbrook	Orpington	10,275(Con.)	17.8 %
William Cash	Stafford	10,151(Con.)	22.7 %
Dame Jill Knight	Birmingham Edgbaston	14,277(Con.)	26.4 %
Peter Griffiths	Portsmouth N	11,418(Con.)	31.3 %
Sir Bernard Braine	Castlepoint	17,999(Con.)	31.7 %
		15,470(Con.)	33.8 %

Offers of help should either be channelled through our office or be made direct to the candidate and constituency. The phone number of the local Conservative Association should be obtainable from Directory Enquiries or, of course, can easily be obtained from Conservative Central Office 012229000. It is important that Conservative Family Campaign is not only seen to be a pressure group putting forward policies but an active part of the Conservative Party when it comes to getting out the vote.

Thirdly, we must make the issues of family life, for which we stand, important in this election. This means each of us raising the issues with the candidates; writing letters to the press; and getting our friends, particularly in Christian organizations, to make it clear to all candidates but in particular the party leaders that their votes will depend upon these fund-amental moral issues.

Thank you very much for all your support, I am sure you will understand that Conservative Family Campaign itself will go into abeyance for the duration of the General Election Campaign. Once we have secured the return of the next Conservative Government then we shall resume our activities, hopefully with an enlarged representation of CFC in the House of Commons.

God Bless you all.

Yours sincerely,
CONSERVATIVE FAMILY CAMPAIGN

raham Webster-Gardiner
airman

Mr Graham Webster-Gardiner
Conservative Family Campaign
45 West Hill Avenue
Epsom
Surrey KT19 8JX.

139 Elm Park Mansions
Park Walk
London, SW10.

21st May 1987.

Dear Webster-Gardiner,

I thank you for your unsolicited letter of 11th May in which
you urge all family folk to pray for Mrs Thatcher in the next few
weeks. Don't tell us, Graham! We're on our knees here from the
early am, scarcely getting up to visit the john or tag a pansy.

Having perused your roneo'd literature I have decided to sub-
scribe substantially towards the fighting fund of Mr Peter Bruinvels
MP (Leicester) who is in the unenviable position of having to hold
on to his seat in a gay lib stronghold. Rather him than me. I enclose £10 towards his campaign costs which I would like you to
'channel' his way and receipt to me.

That said, I have to point out that our correspondence is one-
way traffic at the moment (discounting your roneo'd circulars). You
haven't replied yet to mine of 1st May in which, you may recall, I
informed you that the title of my TV series had been changed from
THE WESTENDERS by HENRY ROOT to CRACK-UP by HENRY ROOT. I further
nudged you re becoming a FRIEND OF CRACK-UP, enclosing a sample of
my new writing paper for your approval, having, as it now does, the
proud slogan at the bottom - 'SUPPORTED BY THE CONSERVATIVE FAMILY
CAMPAIGN'.

Kindly tell me what you think of this when you receipt my
Bruinvels contribution, plus I would like your comments on the odd
behaviour of The Spectator magazine, which dubbed you recently a
crack-pot.

I look forward to hearing from you.

Yours sincerely,

Henry Root

Henry Root.

FILM AND TELEVISION COPYRIGHTS

139 Elm Park Mansions
Park Walk
London SW10

Tel: 01 – 352 9689
Telegrams: Concept London

24th May 1987.

Sir Peter Carey
Morgan Grenfell & Co Ltd
23 Great Winchester Street
London EC2.

Dear Sir Peter,

I am surprised that we have received no reply to the letter sent to you by our Mr Goldfarb (deceased) on 4th May.

I appreciate that you are a busy man, but are you any busier than the Archbishop of York and the Lord Chief Justice, both of whom found time to reply to letters sent to them from our Mr Max Templeton? It's a fine day for law and order, Sir Peter, when the Primate and Lord Chief Justice of England are more punctilious with their correspondence than a City merchant, however distinguished. Is this not an example of the decline in standards which our series deals with?

I now enclose copies of their letters and would particularly ask you for your views on the points raised by the Archbishop, to say nothing of the points raised in the letter to you of 4th May from our Mr Goldfarb (deceased).

I look forward to hearing from you.

Yours sincerely,

Angela Picano

Angela Picano.   Script Editor.

Telephone 01-588 4545
Telex 8953511 MG LDN G
Fax 01-588 5598

From Sir Peter Carey

29th May 1987

MORGAN GRENFELL

Miss Angela Picano,
Script Editor,
H.R. Productions,
Suites 9 - 57,
139 Elm Park Mansions,
Park Walk,
London. SW10.

Dear Miss Picano,

You wrote to me on the 24th of May and, apparently also, on the 7th of May. (I have no trace of receiving this letter).

I do not claim to be busier than the Archbishop of York and the Lord Chief Justice. I do not however wish to comment on the substance of their letters and I see no point in prolonging this correspondence.

Yours sincerely,

Peter Carey

FILM AND TELEVISION COPYRIGHTS

139 Elm Park Mansions
Park Walk
London SW10

Tel: 01 – 352 9689
Telegrams: Concept London

27th May 1987.

Sir Nicholas Goodison
The Stock Exchange
London, EC2N 1HP.

Dear Sir Nicholas,

Further to my telephone conversation of today's date with your secretary, I now enclose a copy of the letter sent to you on 4th May by our Mr Goldfarb (deceased), which, according to your secretary, was shredded by an over-zealous member of your staff before you had a chance to read it.

I look forward to hearing from you.

Yours sincerely,

Max Templeton

Max Templeton. Development Editor.

THE INTERNATIONAL STOCK EXCHANGE OF THE UNITED KINGDOM AND THE REPUBLIC OF IRELAND LIMITED

THE STOCK EXCHANGE

Sir Nicholas Goodison
Chairman

1st June, 1987

Dear Mr Templeton

  You wrote to me on 27th May. I am sorry you have
not had a reply to your letter of 4th May, but as my office
will have told you it was sent to a different address and I
did not receive it. They tell me incidentally that you are
wrong to infer that it was shredded before I was able to see
it. It seems never to have arrived.

  I would want a great deal more information about
your series before being able to agree to being involved:
and at the first reading your letter of 4th May would be
concerned about what appears to be the somewhat sensational
approach. I appreciate that this is often considered
desirable by television editors but I am not keen on this
style myself.

  I have given your correspondence to the Head of my
Public Affairs Department and will ask her to consider it
further in the light of anything further you want to add.

Yours sincerely

Nicholas Goodison

Max Templeton, Esq.,
Executive Producer,
H.R. Productions,
Suites 9-57,
139 Elm Park Mansions,
Park Walk,
London SW10.

Registered Office:
The Stock Exchange, London EC2N 1HP
Telephone: 01-588 2355 Telex 886557
Registered in England & Wales No 2075721

CRACK-UP by HENRY ROOT.

Inter-Office Production Memo.

Date: 2nd June 1987.

Time: 11.33 am.

ZISKIE to McPEAK.

Appended herewith letter from Sir Goodison dated 1st June ult.
I think we've got this turkey, Sandy. Stand by to liase with
the head of his PR affairs. Ready meanwhile a standard PR quest-
ionnaire for completion by Sir Goodison - hobbies, style, most
embarrassing experiences, involvement in previous scandals, is
there nothing he likes more at the end of a hard day than to take
the phone off the hook, put his feet up with a tandoori duck from
a take-away and watch 'Casablanca' of 'The Maltese Falcon' for the
sixteenth time on his video etc? We'll want some deep background
on the man before we put his head on film.

What news on Lindy Benson?

FILM AND TELEVISION COPYRIGHTS

139 Elm Park Mansions
Park Walk
London SW10

Tel: 01 – 352 9689
Telegrams: Concept London

Lord Goodman
Goodman Derrick & Co
4 Little Essex Street
London WC2R 3LD.

26th May 1987.

Dear Lord Goodman,

    You will forgive any faux pas in this letter. Many in our group are from the USA with more pressing matters to attend to than a crash-course in the English way of corresponding or to tog ourselves up in spats and bowlers. Time is money, right?

    Enough of that: here's the story. As the enclosed material will convey, we are engaged here on the development of a TV series of some importance and wish now to appoint you as attorney to the venture.

    Thanks to the antics of two members of our team (one canned, the other deceased), we are already behind the eight-ball here I think. Letters were sent out without safeguards to the Chairman of the Midland Bank, by our ex-Mr Goldfarb, and to Judge Pickles's showbiz agent, Mr Jo Gurnett, by our ex-Development Editor Cox. Here's the question: can the Midland pinch our concept (into Hambro's, showing the cuff: 'Morning Sir Charles, here's the caper....') and can Pickles's agent do the same, Cox having sent an excerpt from the series not marked 'copyright'?

    In order that you may do some preliminary thinking prior to a brain-storming session at your chambers, I now enclose copies of all correspondence with the Midland Bank and also the letters which have passed between this company and Mr Jo Gurnett.

    Do not appoint silks etc yet, but get your metre running. This one could have legs.

    Yours sincerely,

Aaron Seltzer

Aaron Seltzer. Executive Producer.

FILM AND TELEVISION COPYRIGHTS

139 Elm Park Mansions
Park Walk
London SW10

The Secretary
Pratts
14 Park Place
London, SW1.

Tel: 01 – 352 9689
Telegrams: Concept London

26th May 1987.

Dear Sir or Madam,

On the 11th of this month, our Script Editor, Miss Picano
(Italy), wrote to Lord Rothschild on a matter of espionage care of
your club. We have received no reply to this letter and we cannot
help wondering whether you have shredded or otherwise 'lost' it.

I enclose a copy of a copy of Miss Picano's original letter
to Lord Rothschild – which I must ask you to destroy on receipt –
and would warn you of the seriousness of 'tampering' with matters
touching on National Security.

You will see from the final paragraph of Miss Picano's letter
of 11th May that we have arranged to interview Lord Rothschild on
the morning of Tuesday 7th July at your club, but will inform you
at an earlier date as to whether we have any special filming in-
structions for yourselves – closing the premises, laying on canteen
facilities etc.

I look forward to hearing from you with the necessary confirm-
ations etc.

Yours sincerely,

Daniel Ziskie. Producer.

cc.   The Prime Minister.

PRATT'S CLUB,

14 PARK PLACE,

LONDON, SW1A 1LP

Tel. 01-493 0397

From: Captain P W E Parry MBE   10 June 1987

Daniel Ziskie Esq
Executive Editor
Film and Television Copyrights
139 Elm Park Mansions
Park Walk
London S W 10

Dear Sir

Thank you for your letter of 26 May concerning Lord Rothschild's correspondence.

It is our normal practise to forward correspondence to Members, and as far
as I am aware this was done with Ms Picano's letter of 11 May.

I take great exception to the implication in your letter that our staff and
I tamper with mail, and we certainly do not need reminding of the seriousness
of the offence.

In addition, and with reference to the last paragraph of Ms Picano's letter,
may I say that we regard the idea of you carrying out interviews on the Club
premises, either with or without your camera crews, as presumptiousness beyond
description.

Pratts is a proprietary Club and if there is any attempt by any of your employees
to interview on the premises, steps will be taken to remove the offending
persons.

Copies of this correspondence are being lodged with the Proprietor's solicitors,
and any further inference on your part, that the staff are involved in illegal
acts, will be dealt with through the Courts.

Yours faithfully

Secretary

Midland Bank plc

Group Communications and
Public Relations Department
Head Office
Poultry London EC2P 2BX
Telephone 01-260 8000
Extension 38476
Telex 8811822

Direct Line
01-260 8476

Our reference
AAF/MLA

Your reference

M. Goldfarb, Esq.,
Finance Director,
H.R. Productions,
Suites 9-57,
139 Elm Park Mansions,
Park Walk,
London. SW10

52-02

15 May 1987

Dear Mr. Goldfarb,

Your recent letter addressed to our Chairman has been passed to this
department as we are responsible for co-ordinating approaches of this nature.

I have now discussed with our appropriate Department your request for Midland
Bank to support your proposed T.V. series by loaning you the required
development money. I regret to inform you that they have now advised me that
this is not a project that appeals to us and we are unable to assist.

Thank you for allowing us the opportunity to consider your proposal.

Yours sincerely,

Alan Furniss,
Assistant Manager.

Registered in England (No. 14259)
Registered Office Poultry London EC2P 2BX

FILM AND TELEVISION COPYRIGHTS

139 Elm Park Mansions
Park Walk
London SW10

Tel: 01 – 352 9689
Telegrams: Concept London

26th May 1987.

Alan Furniss Esq
Midland Bank plc
Poultry
London, EC2P 2BX.

Dear Mr Furniss,

We are in receipt of your letter of 15th May to our Mr Goldfarb (deceased) and it disappointed us, I must say.

'Efficient - Fair - Courteous' - thus your slogan displayed in high street branches, plus the injunctions 'When you need us, just ask' and 'At all times, if you feel that we have failed, tell us'.

You've failed, Furniss, so I'm telling you. Mr Goldfarb (deceased) wrote to you on 8th May offering you the chance to get in on the ground-floor of CRACK-UP with a minimum investment, and what do we get? A curtly worded turn-down with no reasons given as to why you took a negative line on this one. The least you could have done would have been politely to indicate a fault in our series (artistically) or in our money-raising techniques (many in this group are from the USA and non-cognisant with the English way of passing round the hat).

It would be some assistance to us at this time were you to let us know whether it is the concept which doesn't appeal or the financial side of things. If you would like a bigger share of the cake, just say so. That's the way we do things in America.

Kindly reassure me now that you will not be off down the road passing off our concept as yours and raising the money from the National Westminster or Barclay's (you would eschew Lloyds, I imagine, with that old fool Rumpole and the horse). Don't tell us - we know what happens here. Once was a City gentleman's word was his bond, but post Big Bang and Goodison tourists like us have to watch their backsides. These days, they say, bankers have the morals of black cab drivers with a turkey as a passenger.

I look forward to hearing from you.

Yours sincerely,

Jo Drinkwater.

Dictated by Milton Goldfarb (deceased) and signed in his absence

cc.   Lord Goodman.

Jimmy Smits ~~Milton Goldfarb~~ Alan Rachins Daniel Ziskie Aaron Seltzer Sandy McPeak Jill Eikenberry Jeremy Cox
Angela Picano Max Templeton Julia Mortimer

**Midland Montagu
Ventures Limited**

47 Cannon Street
London EC4M 5SQ

Telephone 01-638 8861
Telex 945241
Fax 01-638 8861

PJG/LCC

12th June 1987

M Goldfarb Esq (deceased)
Finance Director
H R Productions
Suites 9 - 57
139 Elm Park Mansions
Park Walk
London SW10

Dear Mr Goldfarb

Thank you for your letter of 26th May addressed to Mr Furniss.
As Midland Montagu Ventures is the department which considered
your proposal, it has been passed to me to answer.

I am sorry you feel the previous reply fell short of the
standards of courtesy to which you rightly feel you are
entitled. In response to your criticism of the brevity of the
letter, we believe that most clients prefer to have the bad
news (for, of course, that is what it is for them) conveyed as
efficiently as possible and they are often not too interested
in the reasons for the rejection.

However, as you have asked to know the reasons for our
rejection, of course I am glad to assist you. There are
several.

We have carefully considered a number of projects such as yours
over the years but on the evidence of the not very useful
financial statistics produced by the film and TV industry on
its successes and failures, have always concluded that better
risk-reward ratios exist elsewhere in the economy.

I must confess, too, that the concept did not appeal to us very
much. I think you will agree that a decision by a major
British clearing bank to invest in an internationally shown
production highlighting the so-called "moral decline of
Britain" might be regarded by our shareholders as just a bit
provocative, not to mention what effect this would have on the
Government, the City, et al.

Midland Montagu
Ventures provides venture
and development capital
for industry and
commerce and is part of
Midland Montagu, the
investment banking arm
of Midland Bank Group.

Registered in England
No 1268558
Registered Office
27-32 Poultry
London EC2P 2BX

Possibly such an argument may strike you as mealy-mouthed, but you will appreciate that the Midland Bank is a commercial enterprise, with no expertise of, or desire to be involved in, arcane discussions on political history, artistic truth and the secular decline of morals.

I can give you total reassurance that the Midland Bank will not make use of your concept, as we are not involved in the buying and selling of film projects. Any UK Bank regards its client dealings as totally confidential, covered by what is usually called "Bankers' Secrecy". This makes up for the fact that clearing bankers are not really gentlemen.

In view of the large number of proposals we receive which have to be turned down, I regret that it is not our practice to advise clients on how to redraft their proposal into a more acceptable form for presentation to other institutions. May I say though that it is not usually very productive to write direct to the chairmen of the largest corporations with proposals for fairly unimportant sums.

Finally, you may care to know that our very first investment many years ago was in a film-cum-TV project. If my memory serves me correctly (it was a long time ago) it was called "The Henry Root Connection" and it was, alas, a complete flop.

Yours sincerely

John Gater

P J Gater

FILM AND TELEVISION COPYRIGHTS

139 Elm Park Mansions
Park Walk
London SW10

Tel: 01 – 352 9689
Telegrams: Concept London

Mrs Margaret Thatcher
Prime Minister
10 Downing Street
London, SW1.

26th May 1987.

Dear Prime Minister,

CRACK-UP by HENRY ROOT.

As you will have heard, I and my associates from the States
are over here making the above titled TV drama series which will
trace the decline of your country from the swinging Sixties (Mary
Quant) to more recent scandals in the City of London and in the
Tory Party under yourself.

In the course of the past month, our Script Editor, Miss
Picano (Italy), has had occasion to write to Sir Duff of MI5, Lord
Rothschild and Cockfield of Westland Helicopters plc. None has
replied, which strikes us as so odd that we have judged it best
to bring the matter to your attention – touching on National
Security, as it seems to.

I now enclose a copy of our Miss Picano's original letter
to Lord Rothschild – the others were of a similar gist – together
with copies of chasers which we have since sent to the 'cover'
addresses of the three gentlemen involved.

I look forward to receiving your views on this strange state
of affairs.

Cordially yours,

Daniel Ziskie. Producer.

Jimmy Smits Mil⬛⬛⬛⬛⬛⬛⬛an Rachins Daniel Ziskie Aaron Seltzer Sandy McPeak Jill Eikenberry Jeremy Cox
Angela Picano Max Templeton Julia Mortimer

10 DOWNING STREET

From the Principal Private Secretary   29 May 1987

Dear Mr Ziskie,

     I am replying on behalf of the Prime
Minister to thank you for your letter
of 26 May about the letters which your
Script Editor, Ms. Picano, has sent to
various people.

     The correspondence to which you refer
is not something in which the Prime Minister
would want to intervene, but in view of
your reference to the Conservative Family
Campaign, I am drawing to the attention
of the Prime Minister's Political Office
here your question about "tagging" homosexuals
so that they can let you have a reply
on this matter.

Yours sincerely

N. L. Wicks

(N. L. WICKS)

Daniel Ziskie, Esq.

FILM AND TELEVISION COPYRIGHTS

139 Elm Park Mansions
Park Walk
London SW10

Tel: 01 – 352 9689
Telegrams: Concept London

26th May 1987.

Mr Jock Bruce-Gardyne
The Sunday Telegraph
135 Fleet Street
London, EC4.

Dear Mr Bruce-Gardyne,

As you will have heard on the Fleet Street grapevine, this company is making a TV drama/documentary entitled CRACK-UP which will trace the moral decline of this country from the Sixties to Mrs Thatcher's jungle economics. (Here's one. Changing the wheel of my car the other day, I looked up to find a young police constable with his head under the bonnet. When I asked him what his game was, he replied: 'If you're having the wheels, squire, I'm having the battery'. The police in business on their own account, do you see?).

Since I and my associates are from the USA we are concerned that the script we are developing should accurately reflect City usage at the present time, and it has been suggested to us that you might care to act as Technical Adviser on retainer, being au fait, as you are, with politics and money. We would pay you £250 per week to advise on the script and later to make yourself available during shooting in the studio and elsewhere. What do you say to that? Would you as a start kindly advise us as to the correct meaning of the City expressions enclosed hereunder and return?

It might further interest you to know that we are canvassing the moral leaders of this country, seeking their support by becoming FRIENDS OF CRACK-UP. I am not suggesting that supporting us is a Christian obligation - although it is - merely asking your permission to use your name when raising money in the City.

I look forward to hearing from you.

Yours sincerely,

Daniel Ziskie. Producer.

Encs.

GLOSSARY OF CITY TERMS.

Kindly insert where indicated the correct meaning of these terms.

Care for a blow-back?   ....

Bear Hug.   ....

The Powder Room.   ....

Jobbing backwards.   ....

Doing a Fiona Wright.   ....

Doing an Ernest Saunders.   ....

Doing a line in the morning...............

A golden hullo.   ....

Grossing up.   ....

Ambulance stocks.   ....

Crack.   ....

Space-cake.   ....

Yield effective.   ....

Dawn raid.   ....

Bed and Breakfast.   ....

A bell-ringer.   ....

Anyone seen the ammonia?   ....

Anyone seen Jamie?   ....

Hospital tackle.   ....

Tactical payouts.   ....

Back to back.   ....

Concert Party.   ....

Scraping the pipe.   ....

Unusual payments.   ....

Doing a Keith Best.   ....

Bone me up the arse, will you old chappie, ta...............

SUNDAY TELEGRAPH

CITY OFFICE

135 FLEET STREET, LONDON EC4P 4BL   TELEPHONE: 01-353 4242

2nd June, 1987

Daniel Ziskie Esq.,
Exeuctive Produce,
139, Elm Park Mansions,
Park Walk,
London SW10.

Dear Mr. Ziskie,

Thank you for your letter of May 26th about your projected TV series on "the moral decline of this country" over the past 25 years. I am afraid I have never been a great enthusiast for moral crusades on television or in the press - anymore than for immoral ones, if that needs saying. I have always inclined to the view that morality is a matter of private behaviour and personal opinion and I have little more sympathy with those who try to dictate the behaviour of their fellow citizens - so long as that behaviour does not materially damage other fellow citizens - then I have with those who exploit a gullible public. So I am afraid you should really look elsewhere.

Yours sincerely,

Lord Bruce-Gardyne.

28th May 1987

Dear Mr Templeton,

I am replying on behalf of the Lord Chancellor to your
letters of 11th and 24th May. He has asked me to tell you that
he does not want to take part in your series.

With regard to Judge Pickles, the so - called 'Kilmuir Rule'
which applies to all full-time judges, states that it is as a
general rule undesirable for members of the judiciary to broadcast
on the radio or to appear on television. However, this 'rule'
is advisory rather than mandatory and the final decision must be
the Judge himself.

The Lord Chancellor has also asked me to return the £5.00
that you asked him to donate to a charity of his choice.

Yours sincerely

N. A. Oppenheimer

Mrs N A Oppenheimer

Max Templeton Esq
Executive Producer
HR Productions
Suite 9-57
139 Elm Park Mansions
Park Walk
London
SW10

139 Elm Park Mansions
Park Walk
London SW10

Tel: 01 - 352 9689
Telegrams: Concept London

27th May 1987.

Margaret, Duchess of Argyll
The Grosvenor House Hotel
Park Lane
London, W1.

Dear Duchess,

I write to you in connection with a TV series this company is developing – entitled CRACK-UP – which will dramatise many of the scandals of the past two decades. The series will be a skilful blend of fact and fiction and we will introduce a documentary element into the narrative line by filming scenes with many of the people who thought they'd got away with it but haven't. Furthermore, and for the sake of greater authenticity, we have received special permission from Plouviez of Equity – the first time this has been granted, we believe – to employ 'real people' rather than actors to play certain parts which we feel 'artistes' would not have the breeding to carry off (imagine Donald Sinden as old Lord Thornycroft!)

A recent scandal in which we have acquired world-wide TV rights is the so-called Marquis of Beauchamp affair (Judge James Pickles QC has agreed to play the part of Judge Henry Herbert QC, who sat at the disgusting young man's trial) and I wonder whether you might like to play the Part of Beauchamp's mother, the barmy Duchess of Dorset?

If you are interested perhaps you could let me have the name of whoever handles your subsidiary rights. We hope to start filming on location in early August.

I look forward to hearing from you.

Yours sincerely,

Julia Mortimer.

Julia Mortimer. Casting Director.

PS. I enclose a recent picture of the Duchess of Dorset.

Jimmy Smits Milton Goldfarb Alan Rachins D
Angela Pic
erry Jeremy

FILM AND TELEVISION COPYRIGHTS

139 Elm Park Mansions
Park Walk
London SW10

Tel: 01 – 352 9689
Telegrams: Concept London

The Chairman
Harrods
Knightsbridge
London, SW1.

27th May 1987.

Dear Sir,

As you will perceive from the attached confidential correspondence, certain executives of this company have had to involve themselves in matters touching on National Security, such as it is.

We have now been advised that they are themselves at risk, prime targets for retaliatory action by aggrieved MI5 officers (you will be aware of MI5's unenviable worldwide reputation for 'disposing' of those who've crossed its path). In the circumstances I would ask you to lock the attached material in one of your deposit boxes. As the correspondence develops I will send further letters – marked FOR YOUR EYES ONLY – for deposit, and, should one of our executives wake up one morning to find himself upside down in a rubbish skip, I will send you a telegram with the one word 'BOLLARDS'. On receipt of this, you should send the entire correspondence to Detective Chief Superintendent Roy Penrose at New Scotland Yard. He will know what to do with it.

Kindly bill me weekly at the above address.

Yours faithfully,

Aaron Seltzer.

Aaron Seltzer.   Executive Producer.

Encs.

Jimmy Smits Milton Goldfarb Alan Rachins Daniel Ziskie Aaron Seltzer Sandy McPeak Jill Eikenberry Jeremy Cox
Angela Picano Max Templeton Julia Mortimer

FILM AND TELEVISION COPYRIGHTS

Margaret, Duchess of Argyll
The Grosvenor House Hotel
Park Lane
London, W1.

139 Elm Park Mansions
Park Walk
London SW10

Tel: 01 – 352 9689
Telegrams: Concept London

29th May 1987.

Dear Duchess,

On returning to the office today after a girl's lunch with my friend in casting, Selina Sidey, I was informed that you had phoned our Executive Producer, Daniel Ziskie, in a rage, complaining of the fact that I had offered you the part of the barmy Duchess of Dorset in our forthcoming TV series CRACK-UP.

'Never,' you stormed 'have I been so insulted!' My first reaction was: you <u>must</u> have been. My second was: it is <u>I</u> who was insulted, madam. I have been casting internationally for some years now and <u>never</u> have I been accused of insulting anyone by asking them to play a certain role - and, I may say, I have in this time been responsible for the employment of such artistes as Dame Peggy Ashcroft, Lindy Benson and Sir Charles Dance.

What, I must ask you, is so insulting about inviting you to play the key part of the half-mad Duchess of Dorset in our series? I would have offered you the part of yourself, but it is a less good role and since it involves you in a rather squalid scene taking place thirty years ago we have invited Miss Mollie Sugden to play the part. If you would like to be invited, after all, to play yourself, please say so and I will send you the script at once. Miss Sugden has not yet signed a contract.

I look forward to hearing from you and I assure you that your peculiar attitude on the phone will in no way alter my regard for your undoubted professionalism should we still find ourselves working together on this exciting project.

Yours sincerely,

Julia Mortimer

Julia Mortimer. Casting Director.

cc. The Duchess of Dorset.

Lord Goodman
Goodman Derrick & Co
4 Little Essex Street
London WC2R 3LD.

30th May 1987.

Dear Lord Goodman,

I have received as yet no reply to mine to you of 26th May, but I judge it best to bring you up to date with a new development which may, I think, have put us even further behind the eight ball than we were when I wrote on the 26th.

The fact is that our Miss Eikenberry (dismissed) sent out certain passages from CRACK-UP to artistes and celebrities ('Jack' Profumo, Margaret, Duchess of Argyll, 'Lord' Lambton and others who may have got their feet a little muddy) without first having had them read for definition of character or other tort.

We have already heard from the Duchess of Argyll's solicitors re an action (I have informed them that we are represented by you and have asked them to serve due process at your chambers) and I now enclose the passages already submitted here and there by our ex-Miss Eikenberry (USA). I would ask you to have them read immediately for definition, though not by your partner Parrot, if you please. Dr Kit Bryson, author of 'The Naff Calendar 1988' reports that Parrot, invited by Grafton Books to examine this for torts, instead offered his literary opinion (as if anyone wanted that!), pronouncing the enterprise to be in the worst possible taste.

I look forward to hearing from you.

Yours sincerely,

Aaron Seltzer. Executive Producer.

WESTLAND GROUP plc

Hugh P. Stewart
Chief Executive

YEOVIL, SOMERSET,
BA20 2YB.

HPS/MEC/4726

TEL: 0935 702020
FAX: 0935 78846

29 May 1987

Ms. Angela Picano,
Script Editor, H.R. Productions,
Suites 9 - 57, 139 Elm Park Mansions,
Park Walk,
LONDON, S.W.10.

Dear Ms. Picano,

Sir John Cuckney has asked me to reply to your letter of 25 May.

We have no trace of receiving your letter of 8 May and it is not, therefore, surprising that you have not received a response.

Yours sincerely,

FILM AND TELEVISION COPYRIGHTS

139 Elm Park Mansions
Park Walk
London SW10

Tel: 01 – 352 9689
Telegrams: Concept London

Hugh P. Stewart
Westland plc
Yeovil
Somerset BA20 2YB.

1st June 1987.

Dear Mr Stewart,

We are in receipt of your letter of 29th May, informing us that our Miss Picano's letter of 7th May never reached Sir John Cuckney. Following a visit to this office from a 'Major' Randall of MI5 (any info Sir John can give us from the old days on this character would be gratefully received), Miss Picano has disappeared completely! In these circumstances I am sending you a copy of her original letter to Sir John.

Things have moved on a bit since 8th May. Sir Duff of MI5 and Lord Rothschild have sensibly agreed to appear for us on camera, as has that old fraud Peter Wright - the latter's acceptance of our terms meaning that we have to jet out to Tasmania with props, continuity and grip.

A journey to Somerset to see Sir John is no sweat by comparison, and it so happens that on the morning of July 9th we'll be filming at a mad-house in Weston-super-Mare called Broadway Lodge, where we will be exposing the sinister Minnesota Method. This, as you may know, is a behavioural re-programming theory run by Christians whereby junkies are 'cured' by interrogation techniques perfected in North Korea - being repeatedly punched in the stomach while standing in a corner with a bucket on their heads (it works, of course - I'd give up the occasional funny cigarette if that were the penalty!) and we would welcome any comments Sir John - who must be familiar with such methods from his own time as an interrogation officer for MI5 - cares to make.

Anyway - why, if it is convenient for Sir John, don't we kill two birds with one stone, as it were, and shoot Sir John in the afternoon after we've exposed those crack-pot Christians? Unless we hear to the contrary we will arrive at your office with full production facilities at 3pm on 9th July.

I look forward to meeting you then, Hugh.

Yours sincerely,

Daniek Ziskie. Executive Producer.

FILM AND TELEVISION COPYRIGHT

The Chairman
Harrods
Knightsbridge
London, SW1.

139 Elm Park Mansions
Park Walk
London SW10

Tel: 01 – 352 9689
Telegrams: Concept London

1st June 1987.

Dear Sir,

I have not yet had a reply to my letter of 27th May with confidential enclosures for deposit, but I judge it best to send you further correspondence at this time and to bring you up to date with a suspicious development.

I now enclose copies of letters from the Prime Minister and from Sir John Cuckney of the Helicopter Company – odd, I think you will agree, the disappearance of our Miss Picano's first letter to Sir John – plus a copy of our Mr Ziskie's reply to Sir John's jack-in-office.

Kindly deposit these, first taking note of the fact – and memorising it, if you can – that N.L. Wicks of the PM's staff brings up the unpleasant subject of tagging homosexuals at this time although we made no mention of this in our letter to the Prime Minister of 26th May!

Is this a Tory phobia, sir? Have Tories no longer homosexuals under the bed, but on the brain as well? Or are they merely trying to destablise us here with innuendoes?

With regard to the suspicious development: on 28th May in the early pm we discovered a 'Major' Randall sniffing around our outer office and common parts. He had the look of an MI5 operative – stiff upper head, ill-fitting suit, north circular accent – and shortly after his visit our Miss Picano disappeared as completely as her letter of 8th May to Sir John Cuckney!

I must confirm that this isn't yet a BOLLARDS situation (as per my letter to you of 27th May) but I would ask you to report to me w/ immediately should you find a 'Major' Randal sniffing around Haber- dashery or Fish.

We have not yet received an account from you in consideration of your deposit facilities.

Yours sincerely,

Aaron Seltzer. Executive Producer.

Encs.

The Rt. Hon. Margaret Thatcher

32 Smith Square Westminster SW1P 3HH   Tel. 01-222 9000

1st June, 1987

Dear Mr. Ziskie,

Mrs. Thatcher has asked me to thank you for your letter of
the 26thMay and to reply to it and to thank you for your
good wishes.

I have been in touch with the Chairman of the Conservative
Family Campaign and he has positively denied your assertion
that the CFC are touting the suggestion of "tagging"
homosexuals.

From the enclosed correspondence I assume that you are
referring to matters of national security. For day to day
administration of security the Prime Minister relies on the
expertise and specialist knowledge of the Security Services.

Yours sincerely,

DAME ANN SPRINGMAN

Daniel Ziskie, Esq.,
Film and Television Copyrights,
139 Elm Park Mansions,
Park Walk,
london SW10

FILM AND TELEVISION COPYRIGHTS

The Chairman
Harrods
Knightsbridge
London, SW1.

139 Elm Park Mansions
Park Walk
London SW10

Tel: 01 – 352 9689
Telegrams: Concept London

3rd June 1987.

Dear Sir,

Okay – here's the good news. Don't worry about Miss Picano (see my letter of 1st June). She turned up at the office this morning as cool as a cayote having spent a long weekend in Paris with a man who makes jeans for a living. She's of Italian extraction.

Here's the more disturbing news. I enclose a letter for deposit from Prime Minister Thatcher's Political Office. As you can see, Dame Springman <u>yet again</u> drags up this business of tagging homosexuals, which we never mentioned!

Is there, in your opinion, cause for alarm re the Tories's grip on things?

Kindly remit your bill.

Yours sincerely,

Aaron Seltzer

Aaron Seltzer. Executive Producer.

Encs.

FILM AND TELEVISION COPYRIGHTS

139 Elm Park Mansions
Park Walk
London SW10

Tel: 01 – 352 9689
Telegrams: Concept London

Mr Laurence Evans
ICM Ltd
388 Oxford Street
London W1n 9HE.

3rd June 1987.

Dear Mr Evans,

As you will have heard, we are shortly to go into production with a ten-part television series entitled CRACK-UP.

Is Sir John Gielgud available to play the small, but important role of the barmy Duke of Dorset?

If he is available, perhaps you could let me know and I will forward a copy of the script. Our director is familiar with his work and we will not require him to read for the part.

Perhaps you have other artistes who might be suitable for smaller parts - if so, let me know and I will send you a complete cast breakdown.

Yours sincerely,

Julia Mortimer

Julia Mortimer. Casting Director.

J. Gurnett Personal Management Limited

MANAGING DIRECTOR:
J. L. GURNETT

2 NEW KINGS ROAD
LONDON SW6 4SA
Telephone: 01-736 7828
Facsimile: 01-736 5455

29th May 1987.

Jeremy Cox, Esq.,
H.R. Productions,
Suites 9 - 57
139 Elm Park Mansions
Park Walk
LONDON SW10.

Dear Mr. Cox,

Thank you for your letter of 18th May together with dialogue re Judge James Pickles.

Regretfully we find it is not allowable for Judge Pickles to take on an acting part as a Judge in any productions at the present time.

I am sorry therefore that we cannot help.

Yours sincerely,

Jo Gurnett.

Licensed in accordance with the Employment Agencies Act 1973 No. SE 5509
VAT Registration No. 245 3447 63 Company Registration No. 1383908 Registered Offices 16/18 New Bridge Street, EC4.
Any offer contained in this letter does not constitute a contract.

FILM AND TELEVISION COPYRIGHTS

139 Elm Park Mansions
Park Walk
London SW10

Tel: 01 – 352 9689
Telegrams: Concept London

Jo Gurnett Esq
Jo Gurnett Personal Management Ltd
2 New King's Road
London, SW6.

4th June 1987.

Dear Mr Gurnett,

Thank you for your letter of 29th May. I have to tell you that Judge Pickles's sudden, and very unprofessional, 'about-turn' re appearing as Judge Henry Herbert QC in CRACK-UP by HENRY ROOT has put us in a very embarrassing position. Our Miss Mortimer, rather over-zealously perhaps, widely canvassed the news that Pickles was to play the role, and many celebrity/actors subsequently agreed to participate on the strength of his involvement.

In the circumstances, I took the precaution of checking out the matter of Judge Pickles's appearance in the series with the Lord Chief Justice, Lord Lane, and with the Lord Chancellor, old Lord Hailsham.

Lord Hailsham wrote back as follows: 'With regard to Judge Pickles, the so-called Kilmuir Rule which applies to all full-time judges, states that it is as a general rule undesirable for members of the judiciary to appear on television. However, the 'rule' is advisory rather than mandatory and <u>the final decision must be the Judge himself</u>'. (My italics, not Lord Hailsham's).

Overlooking the peculiar English (how can a judge be a final decision?), I think it's perfectly clear that your statement that 'we find it is not allowable for Judge Pickles to take an acting part in any productions at the present time' is not correct.

Lord Justice Lane wrote to us as follows: 'So far as Judge Pickles is concerned, I am sure that your wisdom will dictate the right course for you to take'. Very much suggesting that it is <u>our</u> decision as to whether Pickles will appear, not Pickles's, do you see?

I must now ask Pickles to reconsider his position. If he feels he cannot change his mind perhaps he could at least get us out of the embarrassing position into which he put us by issuing a press announcement to the effect that his change of heart had <u>nothing</u> to do with the quality of the script.

Yours sincerely,

Jeremy Cox. Development Editor.

J. Gurnett Personal Management Limited

MANAGING DIRECTOR:
J. L. GURNETT

2 NEW KINGS ROAD
LONDON SW6 4SA
Telephone: 01-736 7828
Facsimile: 01-736 5455

8th June 1987.

Jeremy Cox, Esq.,
Film and Television Copyrights
139 Elm Park Mansions
Park Walk
LONDON S.W.10.

Dear Mr. Cox,

Thank you for your further letter.

If you would refer to our previous correspondence, you will see that in my
letter I said "before we could indicate Judge Pickles' interest" etc.
I certainly gave no firm indication of interest whatsoever.

Since you ask for further explanation, I will tell you that both the Judge
and I considered the script to be unacceptable in style, content, writing
and characterisation. Judge Pickles also decided that he really felt he
did not want to go into the 'acting' profession and appear in a drama series.
As Lord Hailsham wrote to you, the final decision rests with the Judge himself
and in this case Judge Pickles has declined to take part in the series.

Your Casting person has behaved in a most unprofessional way by taking
our first reponse as a 'yes' pledge and attempting to capitalise on it.

Yours sincerely,

Jo Gurnett (Mrs)

Licensed in accordance with the Employment Agencies Act 1973 No. SE 5509
VAT Registration No. 245 3447 63 Company Registration No. 1383908 Registered Offices 16/18 New Bridge Street, EC4.
Any offer contained in this letter does not constitute a contract.

FILM AND TELEVISION COPYRIGHTS

139 Elm Park Mansions
Park Walk
London SW10

Tel: 01 – 352 9689
Telegrams: Concept London

Sir Peter Carey
Morgan Grenfell Group PLC
23 Great Winchester Street
London EC2 2AX.

3rd June 1987.

Dear Sir Peter,

Thank you for your letter of 29th May 1987. 'I do not claim to be busier than the Archbishop of York and the Lord Chief Justice', you say. I hope you don't claim to be more courteous either.

I come from Italy, Sir Peter, and while I do not claim to be familiar yet with all the manners and ways of this country, I have worked hard, tried to get along in spite of the weather and am proud of the position I have achieved. Never in all the time that I have been here have I received as letter as rude as yours.

I cannot believe that your letter was entirely characteristic so I now enclose a copy of my previous letter, which you say you never received, confident that this will cause you to take a more courteous attitude.

I look forward to hearing from you.

Yours sincerely,

Angela Picano

Angelo Picano. Script Editor.

Morgan Grenfell Group plc

23 Great Winchester Street
London EC2P 2AX

Telephone 01-588 4545
Telex 8953511 MG LDN G
Fax 01-588 5598

From Sir Peter Carey

8th June 1987

MORGAN GRENFELL

Ms Angela Picano,
Film and Television Copyrights,
139 Elm Park Mansions,
Park Walk,
London. SW10.

Dear Ms. Picano,

Thank you for your letter of the 3rd of June and for sending me
a copy of your original letter of the 7th of May.

I am sorry that you found my letter discourteous: no rudeness
was intended. However, now that I have seen your original letter
I must repeat that I see no point in pursuing the matter. I do
not wish to participate in the project you are proposing and have
no comments to offer. In saying this I am not being discourteous,
merely trying to save your time.

Yours sincerely,

Peter Carey

Sir Peter Carey
Morgan Grenfell plc
23 Great Winchester Street
London EC2P 2AX.

25 Albert Avenue
Chingford, E4.

9th June 1987.

Dear Sir Peter,

Thank you for trying to save my time. I'd rather you'd tried
to save my job. Our Managing Director, Mr Jimmy Smits, has dismissed me from the company for upsetting you and now I am a single-
parent mother trying to bring up three children on the dole. The
cat's just died and I haven't had a holiday for six years - but
please don't worry on my account. Just go on making a lot of money
in the City. All it would take from you to get my job back would
be <u>one</u> letter to our Managing Director - but I quite see that that
would be far too much trouble for such a busy man.

I am sorry to have wasted your time again.

Yours sincerely,

Angela Picano

Angelo Picano.

FILM AND TELEVISION COPYRIGHTS

139 Elm Park Mansions
Park Walk
London SW10

Tel: 01 – 352 9689
Telegrams: Concept London

5th June 1987.

Lord Goodman
Goodman Derrick & Co
4 Little Essex Street
London WC2R 3DD.

Dear Lord Goodman,

I have had no reply to my letters of 26th May and 30th May, but I judge it best to bring you up to date immediately with certain developments re our staff, which may result in industrial action by one or both of them.

1. Miss Julia Mortimer. To safeguard our position in the coming action with Margaret, Duchess of Argyll, we have recently suspended Ms Mortimer (Casting) since it was she who wrote the two letters which so upset the Duchess.

B. Miss Angela Picano. She might be a bigger problem. Recently she infuriated Sir Peter Carey of Morgan Grenfell plc, accusing him of discourtesy and then, more seriously, taking a long week-end in Paris with a man who wears an earring and makes jeans for a living. We have dismissed her, of course, and she is now threatening to take the matter up not only with the Italian Ambassador but also with the Commission for Racial Equality (she is from Italy and olive-skinned, you understand) and with the Equal Opportunities Commission.

Kindly advise.

I should further like to take up another matter which is troubling us. In making CRACK-UP we have naturally been in contact with certain people involved in National Security, such as it is. Acting on advice, we took the precaution of sending copies of all correspondence of a sensitive nature to the Chairman of Harrods for deposit in a box. Disturbingly, we have had no reply, and this sensitive material has disappeared completely. Is it, in your opinion, possible that Harrods has 'gone over' - bank, boutique, fish, poultry, haberdashery, Silver Grill and all? The possibility is almost too alarming to contemplate.

I look forward to receiving a reply to this and previous letters at your earliest convenience.

Yours sincerely,

Aaron Seltzer. Executive Producer.

Jimmy Smits Milton Goldfarb Alan Rachins Daniel Ziskie Aaron Seltzer Sandy McPeak Jill Eikenberry Jeremy
Angela Picano Max Templeton Julia Mortimer

COMMISSION
FOR RACIAL
EQUALITY

Elliot House
10-12 Allington Street
London SW1E 5EH

Telephone
01-828 7022

Ms Angela Picano
Film & Television Copyrights
139 Elm Park Mansions
Park Walk
LONDON   SW10

Date   11 June 1987

Our Ref

Your Ref

Dear Ms Picano

RACE RELATIONS ACT 1976

Thank you for your letter of 5 June and enclosures. I would advise you as follows.

You have the right to make a claim to the Industrial Tribunal that you have been the victim of unlawful racial discrimination on grounds of sex and/or race. In this context, "racial grounds" includes race, colour, ethnic or national origin or nationality. The rules of the Tribunal are such that an application should be made within three months of the date of the incident which is the subject of complaint.

The Commission is able to grant assistance to any person who is taking or contemplating legal proceedings under the 1976 Act and if you would like to contact me again I will arrange for an interview here. Please telephone me on 828-7022 extension 360 on or after Tuesday 16 June to arrange an appointment.

I return your photo herewith as you request.

Yours sincerely

ANDREW THOMAS
Senior Complaints Officer

13171

38, EATON PLACE,
LONDON, SW1X 8AN
01-235 9371

CONSOLATO GENERALE D'ITALIA
IN LONDRA

17th June 1987.

Ms Angela PICANO
Script Editor
H.R.PRODUCTIONS
Suites 9 - 57, 139 Elm Park Mansions
Park Walk
LONDON SW10.

Dear Ms. Picano,

Thank you for your letter dated 15th June which, together with the one sent to the Italian Ambassador on the 4th of June, gives me a complete view on the whole matter. It seems to me that maybe there has been a slight misunderstanding between you and Sir Peter Carey about his partecipation to the series entitled 'CRACK-UP".

Although his letter to you could have used a different tone, you will understand that no one is compelled to give his contribution by being filmed or interviewed for a TV documentary.

I am confident that you will be able to find other people for your program and that the Managing Director of your company, Mr. Jimmy Smits, will give you another chance to go on with your project.

Wishing you the best for your future plans,

I remain,

Yours sincerely,

The First Vice Consul
(Giorgio GUGLIELMINO)

cc: Ambasciatore Bruno BOTTAI
AMBASCIATA D'ITALIA
LONDRA

Equal Opportunities Commission
Overseas House
Quay Street Manchester M3 3HN

Telephone 061-833 9244 Ext

**Equal
Opportunities
Commission**

Ms. Angela Picano,
Film & Television Copyrights,
139 Elm Park Mansion,
Park Walk,
London SW10

Your reference

Our reference   87EM 13842/JHC/MO

Date   22nd June 1987

Private & Confidential

Dear Ms. Picano,

Thank you for your letter of 8th June, and the documents
enclosed, which have been passed to me for attention. I
am returning the photographs to you, as requested.

I should explain that the Equal Opportunities Commission was
set up in 1975 to promote equality of opportunity between the
sexes and to monitor the provisions of the Sex Discrimination
Act and the Equal Pay Act.

I have read your correspondence carefully and it appears
that Mr. Seltzer has suspended you because of your correspondence
with Sir Peter Carey and the Italian Ambassador. I note that
you believe that you will be dismissed after an investigation
into your conduct has been carried out. It appears from what
you have said that your complaint would not come under the
provisions of the Sex Discrimination Act as your employer's
actions towards you are not related to the fact that you are
a woman, but to your conduct as an employee, which he considers
to be unacceptable.

In respect of your specific request for information about
whether or not you may have a case for wrongful suspension
from work, I suggest that you contact the Advisory Conciliation
and Arbitration Service (ACAS) whose role to advise on a wide
range of employment legislation. The address and telephone
number of the South East Region office is Clifton House,
83-117 Euston Road, London NW1 2RB. Tel. 01388 5100.

I am sorry that I have not been able to advise you, however
I hope that ACAS will be able to assist you.

Yours sincerely,

JEAN H. CARTER
EMPLOYMENT SECTION

GOODMAN DERRICK & CO.

SOLICITORS

LORD GOODMAN C.H.

J. R. MACKENZIE   J. J. MAUNSELL
J. T. P. ROBERTS   R. M. PERROT
P. G. PERRY   P. L. J. SWAFFER
I. MONTROSE   T. J. LANGTON
DIANA RAWSTRON   G. E. HAMLEN

CONSULTANT
L. C. B. GOWER

9-11 FULWOOD PLACE,

GRAY'S INN,

LONDON WC1V 6HQ

TEL. 01-404 0606

CABLES AND TELEGRAMS : LITSURE, LONDON, W. C. 1
TELEX : 21210 LITLAW G   L. D. E. 122
FAX : 01-831 6407   GROUPS II AND III

YOUR REF   OUR REF   G/CM   DATE   3rd June 1987

Dear Sir,

Lord Goodman has asked me to acknowledge your letter of 30th May and to inform you that he has no recollection of having received any previous letter from you. This may be because it may have been written to Little Essex Street, which this firm left many years ago.

Lord Goodman asked me to say that he much regrets this firm is not able to represent you, for a number of reasons, and especially since one of the persons mentioned is an old and valued client. He asks you to be good enough to write to the Duchess of Argyll's solicitors immediately, informing them that this firm has never acted and is not acting on your behalf, so as to avoid any misunderstanding. We shall be glad to have a sight of the letter you write.

Yours faithfully,

Carolyn Miller

Miss C. Miller
Secretary to Lord Goodman

A. Seltzer, Esq.,
Film and Television Copyrights,
139 Elm Park Mansions,
Park Walk,
London, S.W.10.

Miss Roxanne Vacca
ICM Ltd
388 Oxford Street
London W1N 9HE.

Tel: 01 – 352 9689
Telegrams: Concept London

5th June 1987.

Dear Miss Vacca,

Thank you for phoning about CRACK-UP. It is, as you say, a thrilling project and I now have pleasure in enclosing full synopsis and cast breakdown for your valuable suggestions. Perhaps you could also show copies to Sue in Laurence Evans's office. Laurie is keen that Sir John Gielgud should play the part of the mad Duke of Dorset, and he might have artistes available for other roles. Is Rex Harrison still alive?

Stratford Johns and Anthony Andrews are pressing us hard for the parts of Norman Smallhampton and the coke-sniffing Marquis of Beauchamp, but we have our doubts about both performers. What, off the record, is your opinion of their work? If you have better suggestions for either of these parts, please do let me have them.

A key role which we wish to cast as soon as possible is that of the cabinet minister in Macmillan's government who used to be lowered from the ceiling on a kebab skewer wearing high heels and a suspender-belt. Have you someone ideal for this part? Do you represent Peter Bowles?

If you or Laurie would like to see some draft scenes, do let me know.

Yours sincerely,

Jeremy Cox

Jeremy Cox. Development Editor.

FILM AND TELEVISION COPYRIGHTS

139 Elm Park Mansions
Park Walk
London SW10

Tel: 01 – 352 9689
Telegrams: Concept London

The Secretary
The Parole Board
Queen Anne's Gate
London, SW1 8AT.

6th June 1987.

Dear Sir or Madam,

I have recently had occasion to take action against two associates of this company - one suspended, one dismissed - for what I judged uncorporate behaviour. They are: Miss Angela Picano, who arrived in this company from Naples some twelve years ago - or so she claims - and Miss Julia Mortimer, of whose background I know nothing, I'm glad to say.

I have a feeling that there might be something not quite right about these two ex-executives and I would be grateful if you could run the pair of them through your computer to see whether they both come up brand new, or, to discover, hopefully, that one or other is on parole, on the run, on probation, on drugs or otherwise in trouble. Such info would help us in any coming action and would be paid for generously.

I look forward to hearing from you.

Yours faithfully,

Aaron Seltzer

Aaron Seltzer. Executive Producer.

Abell House John Islip Street London SW1P 4LH

Direct line 01-211
Switchboard 01-211 3000

26 June 1987

Dear Mr Seltzer

I refer to your letter of 6 June addressed to the Secretary of the Parole Board about individuals which you have recently dismissed from your employ.

I am unable to assist you regarding your request for information as this is not a matter in which the Board can properly involve itself.

I return herewith the photograph of Ms Picano.

Yours sincerely

L P LITTLE
Deputy Secretary of the Board

Aaron Seltzer
Executive Producer
Film and Television Copyrights
139 Elm Park Mansions
Park Walk
London SW10

FILM AND

London SW10

Tel: 01 – 352 9689
Telegrams: Concept London

Miss Selina Sidey
Gordon & Ogilvie Ltd
22 Half Moon Street
London, W1.

5th June 1987.

Dear Selina,

I think I'm in a bit of trouble and, though I hate to ask, I wonder if you can help. Aaron is blaming me for upsetting the Duchess of Argyll and is threatening to fire me. He's already fired poor Angela Picano, ostensibly for annoying Sir Peter Carey, but in reality, I think, because she went to Paris with her boyfriend rather than with any of the male chauvenists running this company. I think he wants to get rid of me for much the same reason.

I know Aaron is a friend of the Family and listens to what you say. Could you possibly intervene on my behalf? I'd be huge-ly grateful. I really don't want to lose this job.

Love,

Julia

Telegrams: Casting London

Miss Julia Mortimer
Film And Television Copyrights
139 Elm Park Mansions
Park Walk
London, SW10.

Dear Julia,

6th June 1987.

Don't worry, love. Just leave this to me. If that little Italian firecracker, Miss Picano, had come to me asking for the Family's help - instead of complaining to the Italian Ambassador and God knows who else - she'd still be Development Editor.

I'll have a word with Aaron and be back to you soonest.

Chin up!

Love,

Selina

xx

Telephone: 01-493 7632

GORDON & OGILVIE LTD
22 Half Moon Street
London W1

Mr Aaron Seltzer
Film And Television Copyrights
139 Elm Park Mansions
Park Walk
London, SW10.

Telegrams: Cas...

Dear Uncle Aaron,

6th June 1987.

I've had that dry old stick Julia Mortimer whining on at me. <u>Don't fire her</u>. I spoke to Uncle Joe on the phone last night and he's getting worried about the accident rate among executives. An associate of his at the Italian Embassy in London phoned him yesterday with the news that excitable Miss Picano has already complained to them and is threatening to sue you for wrongful dismissal. Uncle Joe doesn't want any more trouble but has told me to move to your office as Casting Director. I suggest you keep Mortimer on as my assistant - at half salary - to carry the can in case anything goes wrong. Oh - and if she writes any letters I want her to sign them as: Assistant to SELINA SIDEY. That's important.

Uncle Joe is closing down Gordon & Ogilvie immediately and I'll be moving in with you on Monday.

See you all then!

Love,

Selina

e Gord...

FILM AND TELEVISION COPYRIGHTS

139 Elm Park Mansions
Park Walk
London SW10

Tel: 01 – 352 9689
Telegrams: Concept London

The Chairman
The Prudential Corporation
142 Holborn Bars
London EC1 2NH.

7th June 1987.

Dear Sir or Madam,

    I wish to complain about your new TV commercial, featuring the comedian Griff Rhys-Jones and an old street derelict, in which the former twits the latter for not having taken out one of your pension plans. It then turns out that the old derelict has indeed subscribed to you over the years and is now off to the sun on the proceeds with a car-load of bosomy bimbos.

    This insults women, sir, by suggesting that they can be bought by the car-load for a man's pleasure (however old and disgusting the man) and it particularly insults women with large bosoms by suggesting that they are especially susceptible to disgusting old men with pension plans. (On a more trivial level, it insults men too by suggesting that the only reason a man might have for saving through one of your delayed gratification schemes is to enable him in his dotage to take acquiescent and foolish young sex objects to the Costa del Sol). It seems to me quite extraordinary that you should be reinforcing these stereotypes in 1987.

    Such stereotyping is dangerous, as I know to my cost. I am magnificently-bosomed myself, madam, and I was recently put on suspension here for no better reason than this, I believe. The ostensible excuse was that I had insulted Margaret, Duchess of Argyll by offering her the part of the barmy Duchess of Dorset in a TV series I am presently casting for this company, but the <u>real</u> reason, I think, was that our Finance Director, Mr Milton Goldfarb (deceased), had <u>assumed</u> that because of my magnificent bosoms I would be happy to accompany him on a 'location-spotting' trip to the George V Hotel, Paris (the series is to be shot entirely in England) and was most confused, because of my bosoms, when I declined. Thanks to the intervention of my friend in casting, Selina Sidey, I was later reinstated - albeit as her assistant.

    It is conveniently the case that our TV series - CRACK-UP - is precisely about the decline in moral standards brought about by advertisements such as yours. Would you agree to being interviewed on film, apologising for your offensive commercial, perhaps, and confirming that it will be withdrawn as soon as possible?

    I look forward to hearing from you.

    Yours sincerely,

Julia Mortimer

Julia Mortimer. Assistant Casting Director.

CRACK-UP. INTER-OFFICE MEMO.

Date: 9th June 1987.

Time: 5.35pm.

From SELINA SIDEY to Julia Mortimer.

Julia, honey - just seen your letter to the Chairman of the Pru.
It's great - well done! - but the agreement was, as you know, that
you sign all letters as: Assistant to SELINA SIDEY. Sorry to be
heavy about this! We must have lunch some time!

FILM AND TELEVISION COPYRIGHTS

139 Elm Park Mansions
Park Walk
London SW10

Tel: 01 – 352 9689
Telegrams: Concept London

9th June 1987.

Mr Jo Gurnett
J. Gurnett Personal Management Ltd
2 New King's Road
London, SW6.

Dear Jo,

Hi! I'm the new Casting Director on CRACK-UP and I'm sure we'll get on marvellously.

Jeremy Cox, our Development Editor, has passed over to me copies of all previous correspondence, including your most recent letter, and I quite agree with you that our ex-Casting Director Miss Mortimer (now my assistant) was over-zealous when taking Judge Pickles's initial response as a definite 'yes' and by announcing to the media that he was to appear in our series as Judge Henry Herbert QC.

We are disappointed, of course, that Pickles now feels unable to play judges on television and would like instead to suggest the par of the disgusting Mervyn Griffith-Jones QC, prosecuting counsel at the trial of Stephen Ward. I take it that there would be no object- ions from Lord Kilmuir or others to Judge Pickles playing barristers

I look forward to hearing from you and hope very much that Mortimer's rather hysterical behaviour won't have spoilt what I am sure can still be a terrific working relationship between us.

Yours ever,

Selina Sidey

Selina Sidey. Casting Director.

J. Gurnett Personal Management Limited

MANAGING DIRECTOR:
J. L. GURNETT

2 NEW KINGS ROAD
LONDON SW6 4SA
Telephone: 01-736 7828
Facsimile: 01-736 5455

10th June 1987.

Selina Sidey,
Casting Director
Film and Television Copyrights
139 Elm Park Mansions
Park Walk
London S.W.10.

Dear Ms Sidey,

Thank you for your letter of 9th June.

Regretfully Judge James Pickles has decided that he
really does not want to act in any Drama Series. At
the moment we are negotiation several ideas for TV for
him and unfortunately he does not have the time available
to take on any other projects at the present time.

Yours sincerely,

Jo Gurnett.

INTERNATIONAL CREATIVE MANAGEMENT, LTD.

DIRECTORS:
LAURENCE EVANS (CHAIRMAN)
DENNIS SELINGER (MANAGING)
MICHAEL ANDERSON

Jeremy Cox Esq.,
Film & Television Copurights,
139 Elm Park Mansions,
Park Walk,
London SW10.

June 8th, 1987

Dear Jeremy Cox,

RE: "CRACK-UP"

Thank you for your letter of the 5th enclosing details of "CRACK-UP" for which I would like to make the following suggestions:

Fred Smallworthy.......................George Baker/Stanley Meadows

Rita Smallworthy.......................Julia Foster/Angela Douglas

Kevin Smallworthy.......................Chris Milburn

The Duke of Dorset.....................Michael Denison/Terence Alexander

The Marquis of Beauchamp..............Philip Dupuy/Simon Templeman/John Segal

Henrietta.............................Deborah Barrymore

Princess Soszynski....................Suzanne Roquette

I have enclosed the relevant biographies and photographs.

Yours sincerely,

Roxane Vacca

388/396, OXFORD STREET, LONDON, W1N 9HE.   TELEPHONE: 01-629 8080 · CABLE: INCREATIVE.LONDON · TELEX 885974
(REGISTERED OFFICE)   NEW YORK · LOS ANGELES · PARIS · ROME   (REG.NO. 945898 ENGLAND)
EMPLOYMENT AGENCIES ACT 1973 LICENCE NO. SE (A) 2408

A MEMBER OF THE *Josephson* TALENT AGENCY GROUP

FILM AND TELEVISION COPYRIGH

139 Elm Park Mansion
Park Walk
London SW10

Miss Roxanne Vacca
ICM Ltd
388/396 Oxford Street
London W1N 9HE.

Tel: 01 − 352 9689
Telegrams: Concept Lonc

9th June 1987.

Dear Roxanne,

Many thanks for your letter of 8th June with really great
ideas for CRACK-UP.

Your suggestion that George Baker and Stanley Meadows should
both play the part of Norman Smallhampton (formerly Fred Smallworthy)
is good fun but might lead to confusions, I think!

I am reminded of a story in a really terrific book I read
recently called 'Great Theatrical Disasters' (Arthur Barker, £4.85).
In an Old Vic production of Othello in the early Fifties, Richard
Burton and John Neville alternated the parts of Iago, the envious
NCO, and Othello, the jealous Moor. One day, Burton and Neville
lunched theatrically at the Ivy restaurant, emerging eventually
absolutely shit-faced. Remembering that they had a matinee that
afternoon, they struggled back to the theatre and both played Iago!

Your alternative suggestion that Julia Foster and Angela
Douglas should both play Mrs Smallhampton is even sillier, if I
may say so, since Mrs Smallhampton only has one scene. Miss Foster
and Miss Douglas could hardly both appear in that!

I am surprised that you should suggest Michael Denison and
Terence Alexander to alternate the role of the barmy Duke of Dorset.
Surely you must know that Laurence Evans of your office is pressing
us hard to give this part to Sir John Gielgud.

I think Suzanne Roquette looks like a definite possibility
for the part of the nasty little tart Princess Soszynski, and I'll
get back to you on this after I have spoken to our director. Is
Suzanne her real name? It sounds almost too good to be true!

Yours,

Selina Sidey

Selina Sidey. Casting Director.

FILM AND TELEVISION COPYRIGHTS

139 Elm Park Mansions
Park Walk
London SW10

Tel: 01 – 352 9689
Telegrams: Concept London

9th June 1987.

The Rt Hon Cecil Parkinson MP
The House of Commons
London, SW1.

Dear Mr Parkinson,

Hi! I'm the new Casting-Director on CRACK-UP, the exciting TV drama/documentary which will rake up all the scandals of the past twenty-five years. You can run but you can't hide from Film And Telvision Copyrights! Our last Casting Director, Julia Mortimer – now my assistant – kept making the most frightful faux pas!

Anyway, one of the scandals we'll be covering, of course, is the so-called Monica Coghlin Affair and since we are aiming at maximum accuracy at all times it would be a tremendous help to us if you would finally tell the truth and let us know why on earth you paid her to leave the country.

Could you at the same time let me know exactly what your involvement was in earlier scandals – most of which happened before I was even born! – particularly the so-called Profumo, Lambton and Janie Jones Affairs? Having missed most of these, I'm getting into a bit of a muddle, I'm afraid!

I enclose a photograph of Miss Patti Dalton, the actress who will play Monica Coghlin in our series (you may have seen her recently in 'Get Some In' for Thames TV, in which she was really excellent) and hope very much that you may be persuaded to play the part of yourself opposite her. I think the sexual chemistry between you could really burn up the screen!

I look forward to hearing from you.

Yours sincerely,

Selina Sidey. Casting Director.

PATTI DALTON

Jimmy Smits Milton Goldfarb Alan Rachins Daniel Ziskie Aaron Seltzer ~~~~
Angela Picano Max Templeton Julia Mortimer

FILM AND TELEVISION COPYRIGH

139 Elm Park Mansions
Park Walk
London SW10

Tel: 01 – 352 9689
Telegrams: Concept London

9th June 1987.

Jeffrey Archer Esq
93 Albert Embankment
London, SE1.

Dear Mr Archer,

You will already have heard on the literary/showbiz grapevine
that this company is making a really super ten-part TV drama/document-
ary, entitled CRACK-UP, which will trace the moral collapse of this
country from the Sixties (Caroline Coon) to more recent scandals in
the City of London and in the Tory Party under Mrs Thatcher.

You'll be glad to hear that one recent scandal we'll be dealing
with is that involving yourself and Miss Sara Keays. Since we're
aiming at maximum accuracy when depicting 'real' people, I wonder
whether you would like to check the details of a rather touching scene,
already written, featuring yourself and Ms Keays? Let me know and I'll
send it off to you immediately.

Could you at the same time let me know what your involvement,
if any, was in earlier scandals - most of which happened before I was
born! - particularly the so-called Profumo, Lambton and Janie Jones
Affairs? I know you resigned once after some awful smell but I can't
remember why.

I enclose a photograph of a Miss Jan Younger, an excellent
actress who will play Miss Keays in our series (you may have seen
her recently in 'Cabaret' at the Manor Rep, Sidmouth) and I hope very
much that you may be persuaded to play the part of yourself opposite
her. The sexual chemistry between you would be quite something!

I look forward to hearing from you.

Yours sincerely,

Selina Sidey

Selina Sidey. Casting Director.

JAN YOUNGER

Jimmy Smits ~~Milton Goldfarb~~ Alan Rachin
Angela
Jeremy Cox

FILM AND TELEVISION COPYRIGHTS

139 Elm Park Mansions
Park Walk
London SW10

Tel: 01 — 352 9689
Telegrams: Concept London

Cecil Parkison MP
The House of Commons
London, SW1.

19th June 1987.

Dear Mr Parkinson,

Oh my goodness! What can I say? In my letter to you yesterday I completely confused you and Jeffrey Archer. _Please_ forgive me - but you must understand that to girls of my age all you old Tories look the same!

I now enclose a copy of the letter I wrote to Mr Archer and would ask you to substitute yourself for him, answering, if you would, the questions that I put to him (now you) about Miss Sara Keays (what a sour-faced old bat _she's_ turned out to be!)

I also enclose a copy of the scene featuring you and Miss Keays, confident that you'll want to play yourself in the series once you've read it.

With a _million_ apologies.

Yours sincerely,

Selina Sidey. Casting Director.

Enc. CRACK-UP. Episode 6, Scene 1.

CRACK-UP. Episode 6. Scene 1. INTERIOR. The Westminster love-nest of the Rt Hon CECIL PARKINSON MP. There are signed photographs of Mrs Thatcher, 'Tiny' Rowland, Virginia Mayo and Jeffrey Archer on the walls. Present: CECIL PARKINSON and SARA KEAYS, a bitter, unattractive single woman in her early thirties. PARKINSON is standing in front of a department store mirror, pulling faces.

SARA KEAYS: What are you doing Cecil?

PARKINSON: I'm practising a sense of humour, Sara.

SARA KEAYS: A sense of humour? What do you mean?

PARKINSON: It's the new thing. You can take a course in it. 'How to Show A Sense Of Humour - A Twelve-Part Course For People In The Public Eye'. The PM's done it. And Jeffrey Archer. And Max Hastings. He failed, actually. Archer passed on the sixth attempt. It's jokes, do you see?

SARA KEAYS: Jokes? What jokes?

PARKINSON (looking unhappy): All kinds of jokes. People make them. On this course we learn how to recognise the damn things. It's not easy, I can tell you. It's run by some fellow called Brandreth. Apparently he's got a sense of humour.

SARA KEAYS: Isn't that what Sarah Ferguson's got?

PARKINSON: I think so, yes. Anyway, this fellow Brandreth wears a canary yellow sweater with a penguin on it and he does funny voices.

SARA KEAYS: Is that a joke?

PARKINSON: What?

SARA KEAYS: The penguin.

PARKINSON: Perhaps it is. I don't know. I told you it wasn't easy. When someone makes one of these joke things, you're supposed to smile. Like this.

(PARKINSON draws back his lips like a shark showing its teeth to a gum specialist).

SARA KEAYS: Oh! That's <u>horrible</u>!

PARKINSON: I know, But it's the new thing, I tell you. We learn how to make them too - these joke things. Yesterday it was the PM's turn. Brandreth taught her a joke and then made her repeat it until she got it right.

SARA KEAYS: What joke?

PARKINSON: It went something like this: At the last Labour Party Conference Neil Kinnock was up all night conferring with his chief policy adviser. When he came down to breakfast the next morning, Roy Hattersley, who's got a sense of humour, apparently, said: "Ah! Moses comes down from the mountain with the tablets!"

SARA KEAYS: Is that the joke?

PARKINSON: Not yet. At this point, Brandreth told the PM to say: "Keep taking the tablets, Neil!"

SARA KEAYS: Oh.

PARKINSON: But the PM kept saying: "Keep taking the pills, Neil." She couldn't see the difference. She thought her version was better, in fact.

SARA KEAYS (looking puzzled): Isn't it?

PARKINSON: I don't think so - not according to Brandreth, anyway. Archer and Hastings agreed with the PM, but Brandreth insisted that he was right. He couldn't budge the PM, however. At the next Tory Party Conference, she's going to say: "Keep taking the pills, Neil".

SARA KEAYS (uncertainly): Ha! Ha!

PARKINSON: That's right. Ha! Ha! You've got the hang of it already. I don't know why Max Hastings failed. I think he makes very good jokes.

SARA KEAYS: Like what?

PARKINSON: He's got a labrador bitch. He calls it 'Jill Tweedie'. Ha! Ha!

SARA KEAYS: Ha! Ha! I like this. Tell me another joke.

PARKINSON: All right. Here's one we learnt today. A Scotsman tells a joke to another Scotsman. It goes like this: A Scotsman gets to heaven but St Peter won't let him in. It's not worth making porridge for one, says St Peter.

SARA KEAYS: Nor it is.

PARKINSON: I'm not finished yet. The second Scotsman doesn't laugh.

SARA KEAYS: I'm not surprised.

PARKINSON: So the first Scotsman tells a third Scotsman how his joke failed with the second Scotsman. The third Scotsman says: "You could na' get a joke into a Scotsman's head except wi' a rivet-gun". So a fourth Scotsman, who happens to be listening, says: "Aye, but you could na' doo that. It would kill the wee laddie."

SARA KEAYS: Well, of course it would. That's just silly.

PARKINSON: <u>Exactly</u>. I told you it was confusing. But we've all got to do it - learn this sense of humour thing. The PM insists. She thinks it may be an Election issue.. Compassion initiatives and a sense of humour. To coincide with the riot season.

SARA KEAYS: Well - I've got a joke.

PARKINSON: Good heavens. What?

SARA KEAYS: I'm pregnant.

PARKINSON: Oh my God!

SARA KEAYS: I thought you'd like it.

PARKINSON: But my career! I'll have to abandon you! I must go
back to my fragrant wife at once, be photographed with her standing
by me in a country churchyard! I'll wear Wellington boots and
carry a stick, walk a labrador across muddy fields, the whole family
trailing behind, smiling bravely. Good-bye forever, Sarah!

(PARKINSON exits).

RICHARD WEST: She was just a political football.

MARY KENNY: Womanizers dislike women, of course, and at bottom
are afraid of them.

FADE.

139 Elm Park Mansions
Park Walk
London SW10

Tel: 01 – 352 9689
Telegrams: Concept London

10th June 1987.

Mr Jeffrey Archer
93 Albert Embankment
London, SE1.

Dear Mr Archer,

Golly golly silly me! <u>Please</u> ignore my letter to you yesterday
in which I quite confused Sara Keays and Monica Coghlin, thinking you
were 'involved' with the former and Mr Cecil Parkinson with the latter!
I now enclose the letter I wrote to Mr Parkinson about Ms Coghlin
(with photograph of the actress playing her) and hope that you will
still be keen to play the part of yourself opposite her in our series.
And we would still like to know why you paid her to leave the country.

<u>Terribly</u> sorry!

Yours ever,

Selina Sidey.

Selina Sidey. Casting Director.

Jeffrey Archer

11 June 1987

Ms Selina Sidey
Film and Television copyrights
139 Elm Park Mansions
Park Walk
London SW10

Dear Ms Sidey,
Many thanks for your letter of 10 June.

As the matter is subjudice with two court cases pending
I am not in a position to make any comments.

Yours Sincerely
Jeffrey Archer

Vincent Shaw Esq
20 Jay's Mews
London, SW7.

London SW10

Tel: 01 – 352 9689
Telegrams: Concept London

10th June 1987.

Dear Vincent,

Hi! I'm the new Casting Director on CRACK-UP, the exciting ten-part TV series which will rake up all the scandals of the past twenty-five years. You can run but you can't hide from Film And Television Copyrights!

Many of the people involved in these scandals will, as you may have heard, be taking part - played either by themselves (unless they're past it!) or by actors and actresses (Janie Jones will be played by herself, Margaret, Duchess of Argyll by an actress).

We will of course be covering the so-called Profumo Affair (I wasn't even born, but I expect you remember it well!) and we are now wondering whether Miss Mandy Rice-Davies, whom I'm told you 'represent', thinks she could still get away with appearing as herself, or, if not, whether she would like to advise us on a suitable actress to play her. We would also, of course, welcome her advice on the scenes in which she is featured since we wish to achieve as much accuracy as possible. Perhaps she would like us to send her a script of these passages so that she can judge them herself for authenticity.

It occurs to me that you might represent other 'artistes' suitable for similar parts. If this is so, do please let me know and I'll rush you over a cast breakdown abd synopsis of the whole series.

Really looking forward to hearing from you, Vincent.

Yours sincerely,

Selina Sidey

Selina Sidey.

FILM AND TELEVISION COPYRIGHTS

139 Elm Park Mansions
Park Walk
London SW10

Tel: 01 – 352 9689
Telegrams: Concept London

10th June 1987.

Miss Sara Randall
Saraband Associates
265 Liverpool Road
London N1 1LX.

Dear Sara,

Would your clever client Julie Walters like to play the part of Margaret, Duchess of Argyll in our new ten-part TV drama/documentary CRACK-UP which will start shooting in September?

Okay - it might seem a kooky piece of casting on the face of it, but the Duchess is, as you probably know, the daughter of a self-made man from the north and we want to emphasise how common she really is. If Julie is free, perhaps you could let me know soonest.

Do you by any chance handle Maureen Lipman as a writer? I think her humour's really zany (loved her latest book with a picture of her on the front sitting on a chamber-pot!) and I wonder whether she'd like to look at a couple of scenes from CRACK-UP with a view to her injecting a bit of her irreverent, whacky humour?

I look forward to hearing from you.

Yours,

Selina Sidey

Selina Sidey. Casting Director.

Saraband Associates

265 Liverpool Road, Islington, London N1 1LX. Telephone: 01-609 5313/4
Sara Randall : Bryn Newton

Miss Selina Sidey,
139 Elm Park Mansions,
Park Walk,
London S.W.10.

11th June 1987

Dear Miss Sidey,

Thank you for your letter. At the moment I can't tell you about
JULIE WALTERS availability in September because we are awaiting a
go ahead for a film to start in August. However, if you could
let me know specific dates in September I might be able to be more
helpful. Her film "Buster" begins shooting on or about 28th September.

I have pleasure in enclosing a list of clients and would be delighted
to arrange for you to meet anyone whom you do not already know and
could perhaps suggest more specific casting if I could see a character
breakdown.

I am afraid MAUREEN LIPMAN is not available this year but thank you
very much for thinking of her.

If you think it would be a good idea for us to meet perhaps we could
have lunch during the week of 22nd or 29th June - I am on holiday next
week.

Yours sincerely,

SARA RANDALL

Registered in England No. 1141148. Registered Office: Waterman House, Chertsey Road, Woking, Surrey.
Saraband Associates is the registered trade name of Shepherdswell Productions Limited
Directors: S. Randall : B. Newton : N. Smyth : Employment Agents Act 1973 Licence No. SE(A)4080.
V.A.T. Registration No. 234 8538 48

VERA CHRISTIE and CHUCK JULIAN AGENCY

Cecil House, 3rd Floor 41 Charing Cross Road, London WC2H OAR
Telephone: 01-437 4248/5380

VAT No: 368 4803 20

11th June 1987

Licence No: SE8813

Julia Mortimer
Film and Television Copyrights
139 Elm Park Mansions
Park Walk
London   SW10

Dear Julia,

Re: "CRACK UP"

Further to Chucks recent suggestions for your production, please now find
enclosed photos with C.V.s of some really interesting faces and talented
actors for bit parts and cameos. I have sectioned them all to make it
quicker and easier for you to go through.

I look forward to hearing from you.

Kind Regards,

Karen

Karen Yager
VERA CHRISTIE & CHUCK JULIAN AGENCY

Enc.

VERA CHRISTIE and
CHUCK JULIAN AGENCY

Cecil House, 3rd Floor 41 Charing Cross Road, London WC2H OAR
Telephone: 01-437 4248/5380

VAT No: 368 4803 20   Licence No: SE8813

PROSTITUTES AND LESBIANS

PATTI DALTON   LEA ROCHELLE
LAURA FAUSNER   LISA WOOD
GIL BERESFORD   SCARLET FLEMMING
JACQUELINE DAVIS   SUE UPTON
LINDSEY LOMAX   MARIA VENTURA
JODY SCHALLER   STEFANIE MARRIAN

GOSSIP COLUMNISTS

SHIRLEY GREENWOOD
JUNE LEWIS
NORMA DUNBAR

SLOANE RANGERS AND OLD HARROVIANS

CHERYL PAY   GRAHAM WYLES
DEBBIE RADCLIFFE   PETER MANTLE
TOBINA MAHON BROWN   JEREMY TRUELOVE
                     JONATHAN FRYER
JUNKIES   PAUL GODDARD
                     CLIVE JOHNSTONE
GORDON WINTER
ROBERT MARTIN
MARY CHATER
CHRIS HALE

COUNSELLORS IN DRUG CLINICS

JAN YOUNGER
KATE MICHELL
GILLIAN PHELPS
ANDREW BLAIR

MEMBERS OF KGB

PETAR VIDOVIC
BRETT FORREST
JULIAN BATTERSBY
MARTIN HEAD

CENTRAL DRUG SQUAD

JONATHAN FRYER
JULIAN BATTERSBY
TERRY COWLING
PATRICK FRENCH
BRETT FORREST
TIM KIRBY

BLACK GIRLS

DEIRDRA LOVELL
JOAN HOOLEY

COMMODITY BROKERS

EDMUND DRING
CRISPIN DE NYS

MEMBERS OF PERSONAL MANAGERS' ASSOCIATION

FILM AND TELEVISION COPYRIGHTS

Graham Webster-Gardner Esq
45 West Hill Avenue
Epsom
Surrey, KT19 8JX.

139 Elm Park Mansions
Park Walk
London SW10

Tel: 01 – 352 9689
Telegrams: Concept London

11th June 1987.

Dear Webster-Gardner,

I am astonished that I haven't had a reply to my letter of
21st May - not so much for the discourtesy in not answering but for
trousering the £10 I enclosed, which, as I made clear in my letter,
wasn't for you, but for Mr Peter Bruinvels MP. Imagine my embarrass-
ment when, having shafted Bruinvels by mail - upbraiding him for not
acknowledging receipt of same - he wrote back saying he'd never
received it!

I must admit that in my anger I put the matter in the hands
of my solicitor, Mr Peter Carter-Ruck, and he has advised me to
bait the hook again, as it were, by sending another tenner, hoping
that this one at least ends up with Bruinvels.

I still look forward to hearing from you re the points raised
in my previous letters and enclose a copy of a recent letter from
the Bishop of London, which suggests, I think, that top churchmen
find time to deal with their correspondence.

I'm praying for a Tory victory today, as I am sure you are.

Down on your knees for Mrs T!

Henry Root.

Henry Root.

cc.   Mr Peter Bruinvels MP.

Vincent Shaw Esq
20 Jay's Mews
London, SW7.

139 Elm Park Mansions
Park Walk
London SW10

Tel: 01 – 352 9689
Telegrams: Concept London

12th June 1987.

Dear Vincent,

A million apologies for being out of the office having my hair done when you telephoned yesterday. Life must go on - even when casting a TV soap!

Anyway - I now enclose a scene from Episode 3 of CRACK-UP between Mandy Rice-Davies and a Tory property developer called Peter Rachman (who on earth was he?). Mandy has three other brilliant scenes - two with Christine Keeler and one with a county court judge who likes her to encase him from head to toe in plaster of Paris (aren't men pathetic?!?) These scenes are now being reworked by our writing-team in the South of France, but I will forward them to you as soon as possible.

I would particularly like to emphasise that none of Mandy's scenes contains any explicit language or nudity whatsoever, unnecessary or otherwise.

I also enclose a synopsis and cast breakdown of the whole series and look forward to receiving any other suggestions you may have. We are particularly keen to find someone to play the senior minister in Macmillan's government who at cabinet meetings was lowered from the ceiling on a kebab skewer. Do you by any chance represent Sir John Mills?

With very best wishes,

Selina Sidey

Selina Sidey. Casting Director.

Enc. CRACK-UP, Episode 3, Scene 4.

CRACK-UP. Episode 3, Scene 4. INTERIOR. Murray's Cabaret Club in Beak Street, Soho. Early evening. Present: PETER RACHMAN, a Tory property developer, MANDY RICE-DAVIES, a high-spirited call-girl and society wit, the KRAY TWINS, the GREAT TRAIN ROBBERS, LORD ASTOR, BARBARA WINDSOR, KGB AGENTS, and various PUNTERS, HOSTESSES, WAITERS, BOGGLERS, BARMEN, etc.

MANDY RICE-DAVIES: Fucking hell I'm really pissed off. This place is full of cunts.

MAX HASINGS: Four letter words are a sign of an impoverished vocabulary.

GEOFFREY WHEATCROFT: Old Bill Shakespeare didn't need to use four-letter words.

RACHMAN (approaching MANDY RICE-DAVIES): Say the word, sweetheart, and you and I could happen.

MANDY RICE-DAVIES: Uuurrgh! You're a man quick-sand would spit up!

RACHMAN: Is that a 'yes'?

MANDY RICE-DAVIES: What! I'd rather be the love-toy of a Greek infantry battalion!

GEOFFREY WHEATCROFT: Who wouldn't? But dreaming will get her nowhere.

RACHMAN: Show me your tits, then.

CHRISTOPHER BOOKER: She's on a slippery slope.

MARY KENNY: This is the M1 to loneliness.

IRMA KURTZ: Yet paradoxically women have earned the right to do what they like with their own bodies.

RACHMAN: Go on, then.

MANDY RICE-DAVIES: Okay.

(She removes her top).

RONNIE BARKER: My word! You wouldn't get many of those to the pound!

RICHARD WEST: There's nothing wrong with a bit of healthy English vulgarity - something which so-called intellectuals of the Guardian-reading sort have still to understand.

NORMAN TEBBIT: The permissive values of the Sixties were never embraced by the man at the pub bar. The chap who enjoys looking at Page 3 of The Sun is the same as his so-called superior on the Holland Park cocktail circuit who looks at the nudes at the National Gallery and say how well they are painted. It's the Sun-reader at the pub bar who supports family life and fights the permissive society.

RICHARD INGRAMS: I concur. Yet when TV producers run out of ideas they try to shock us with pictures of war atrocities and naked women.

MANDY RICE-DAVIES: It's <u>Mrs</u> Ingrams I feel sorry for.

(She takes off all her clothes).

ANNA RAEBURN: Ponder and weep.

FADE.

20 JAY MEWS, LONDON SW7 2EP Telephone 01-581 8215

15th June 1987.

Ms. Selina Sidey,
Film & Television Copyrights,
139 Elm Park Mansions,
Park Walk,
S.W.10

Dear Selina Sidey,

Thank you for sending us the synopsis and cast breakdown of
CRACK-UP.

We are sending the scene from Episode 3 to Mandy Rice-Davies
and will let you have her comments when she returns from
Miami, which we expect to be on June 20th.

Meanwhile we have pleasure in enclosing suggestions for a
few of the other characters.

With best wishes.

Yours sincerely,

VINCENT SHAW.

Director Vincent Shaw   Registered in London No.
Registered Office 20 Jay Mews, London SW7 2EP.
Licensed in Accordance with the Employment Agencies

20 JAY MEWS, LONDON SW7 2EP Telephone 01-581 8215

15th June 1987.   <u>Suggestions for "Crack-Up"</u>

We enclose details of all clients suggested.

For the part of:-

Rita Smallhampton ...... JULIETTE KAPLAN. Plays Pearl in
                        "Last of the Summer Wine", BBC,
                        with a north country accent, though
                        she is in fact a Londoner.
                        Juliette is an excellent actress and
                        would be very good in this part.

Tracey Smallhampton .... AMANDA GOVEY. Talented and professional
                        young actress. She had a scene with
                        James Bolam as the rather stroppy,
                        streetwise Wanda in "Father Matthew's
                        Daughter", of which we have a video,
                        but she would be just as effective being
                        quiet and studious.

The Duke of Dorset ..... GUY ROLFE. Currently the Emperor in
                        "William Tell" for Crossbow Films,
                        Guy is at his best playing eccentric
                        aristocrats.

Princess Soszynski ..... NINKA SCOTT. She is NOT irresistably
                        beautiful, but she is half Polish (she
                        speaks the language) and has a tremendously
                        sexy quality. We thought her worth
                        mentioning.

Lord Denning .... CHARLES SIMON. He has met Lord Denning
                        and reckons he could play him, particularly
                        as Lord Denning has a Gloucestershire
                        accent and Charles is native Gloucestershire.

Director Vincent Shaw Registered in London No 748046
Registered Office 20 Jay Mews, London SW7 2EP
Licensed in Accordance with the Employment Agencies Act, 1973. No. SE(A) 390

FILM AND TELEVISION COPYRIGHTS

139 Elm Park Mansions
Park Walk
London SW10

Tel: 01 – 352 9689
Telegrams: Concept London

Mrs Maggie Parker
Al Parker Ltd
Flat 125
55 Park Lane
London W1.

15th June 1987.

Dear Maggie,

Thank you for phoning the office today. You will forgive me for not having heard of Lindsey Anderson - none of us here has much time to watch television. Your reported reaction to the synopsis - 'My God! This is Lindsey!' - was what we like to hear, however, so if you'd like to bike me round his credits I'll have a think and then, perhaps, let you see the script.

I look forward to hearing from you.

Yours sincerely,

Danile Ziskie. Producer.

FILM AND TELEVISION COPYRIGHTS

139 Elm Park Mansions
Park Walk
London SW10

Tel: 01 – 352 9689
Telegrams: Concept London

Mrs Al Parker
Al Parker Ltd
Flat 125
55 Park Lane
London, W1.

16th June 1987.

Dear Maggie,

Thank you for phoning again. You sounded a little depressed - but I expect you're under a lot of pressure. Okay - we'll give Lindsey the chance to read the script. I must stress, however, that we're entering into no commitment at the moment.

All the best,

Daniel Ziskie. Producer.

Enc. CRACK-UP, Episode 1, Scene 1 and Episode 5, Scene 9.

CRACK-UP. Episode 1. Scene 1. INTERIOR. The SMALLHAMPTON's lounge-diner in their ranch-style duplex at the right end of Acton Avenue. There is a plum velvet three-piece suite and a cocktail cabinet in the form of a crouching Atlas with a globe on his shoulders (a wedding present from their good friends the Michael Parkinsons). On the fake grand piano there are signed photographs of Lee Trevino, Lennie Bennett, Ernie Wise and Paul Raymonde. Present: NORMAN SMALLHAMPTON, RITA SMALLHAMPTON, his wife, and KEVIN SMALLHAMPTON, their son. Early morning. Enter TRACEY SMALLHAMPTON (19), their daughter.

TRACEY: Good morning everyone.

KEVIN: Good morning Tracey.

NORMAN SMALLHAMPTON: Good morning Tracey.

RITA SMALLHAMPTON: Good morning Tracey.

TRACEY: Well everyone. I'd better be off now. This is my first day studying Sociology and Vitamins at Essex University. Goodbye then.

RITA SMALLHAMPTON: Goodbye.

NORMAN SMALLHAMPTON: Goodbye.

KEVIN: Good luck!

TRACEY: Thank you everyone!

(TRACEY EXITS.)

KEVIN: Well, I'd better be off too. This is my first day at Grenfell Morgan Lazards Carey and Collier & Co plc, a well-known merchant bank and futures commodity house in the City of London.

NORMAN SMALLHAMPTON: Goodbye then son. Work hard!

KEVIN: I will, dad. I won't let you down. But for you I wouldn't have been able to get fifteen 'A' levels and a job in the City.

RITA SMALLHAMPTON: Goodbye son!

KEVIN: Goodbye! See you tonight!

(KEVIN EXITS).

RITA SMALLHAMPTON: I can't help feeling proud, Mr Smallhampton. Only twenty-one and already earning £150,000 a year plus Porsche.

NORMAN SMALLHAMPTON: At this age, Mrs Smallhampton, I was earning five shillings a week working day and night on the family eel stall, later sold to me on his death-bed by my dear grandfather, 'Cannonball' Smallhampton. It was three-to-a-shirt in those days and the outside bucket, but I worked hard, saved hard.....

RITA SMALLHAMPTON: Yes yes, Mr Smallhampton. Well, I'm off now to my weekly karate class.

(NORMAN SMALLHAMPTON WHACKS MRS SMALLHAMPTON HARD ON THE BACK OF THE NECK. SHE GOES DOWN LIKE AN OX IN AN ABATTOIR).

NORMAN SMALLHAMPTON: Ha! Ha! I told you, Mrs Smallhampton - a fat old man will always beat a fat old woman.

RITA SMALLHAMPTON (recovering slowly and getting to her feet): A lesson I've yet to learn, Mr Smallhampton!

NORMAN SMALLHAMPTON: Well, I'm off to check on my high street leases. Have a good day!

RITA SMALLHAMPTON: Thank you, Mr Smallhampton. And don't be late. It's kippers for tea.

FADE.

CRACK-UP. Episode 5. Scene 9. INTERIOR. NORMAN SMALLHAMPTON's
ranch-style duplex at the right end of Acton Avenue. Present:
NORMAN SMALLHAMPTON and RITA SMALLHAMPTON. SMALLHAMPTON is pacing
up and down, looking out of the window and moaning quietly to
himself like a moose in a trap. Early afternoon.

SMALLHAMPTON: God help us, Mrs Smallhampton, the world's gone mad,
I say! The skies are dark with flying pigs and Sir Peter Carey
neglects his correspondence. Men dance together in the street and
women give birth in Safeways. Once was a man could leave his boots
outside the door knowing they wouldn't be nicked. Not anymore.
My legs have turned blue, the boy's on drugs, the girl's in
Catering.....

RITA SMALLHAMPTON: Vitamins, Mr Smallhampton.

SMALLHAMPTON: The boy's on drugs, the girl's on Vitamins.....

RITA SMALLHAMPTON: And I'm off to start a new life with Viscount
Weymouth, Mr Smallhampton.

(RITA SMALLHAMPTON exits with her suitcase.)

SMALLHAMPTON: Well I'll be blowed! Never mind. I'll form
Fathers Anonymous! I'll call on the half-mad Duke of Dorset!
I'll move mountains, overcome tremendous obstacles, be drugged
and compromised by MI5, I'll clean up the country on my own!
I'll pray with the PM, meet the Queen, have an affair with
Princess Michael of Kent, receive a peerage from a grateful
nation, dance with Geoffrey Wheatcroft.....

FADE.

FILM AND TELEVISION COPYRIGHTS

139 Elm Park Mansions
Park Walk
London SW10

Tel: 01 – 352 9689
Telegrams: Concept London

Miss Sara Randall
Saraband Associates
265 Liverpool Road
London N1 1EX.

16th June 1987.

Dear Sara,

Many thanks for your letter of 11th June about Julie Walters. I understand that Julie starts shooting 'Buster' on or about 28th September, but I wonder if you could let me know how long shooting may last. The way things are going here, we might not be ready till the new year! We'd really like to have Julie if it's at all possible.

You say that Maureen Lipman is fully booked this year, but did you realise that it was for her witty writing that we wanted her rather than for her humorous acting?

I'm enclosing now a synopsis of the series together with a full cast breakdown and selection of draft scenes so that you can suggest artistes for other parts. The <u>really</u> brilliant news is that the whole script is undergoing a re-write by Nicholas Coleridge of Harpers Queen! We're immensely excited by this because <u>no one</u> knows more about this sort of thing than Nicholas.

Hey - I noticed on your client list that you represent Lynda Lee-Potter. I just adore Lynda's work and we've been wondering whether to ask her to carry out some re-writes on bits that are outside Nicholas's experience - the glitzier world of media and showbiz celebrities which Lynda knows better than anyone. Could I take you and Lynda out to lunch to talk about this? Let me know when you might both be free and I'll book us a table at Langans.

I very much look forward to hearing from you, Sara.

Yours sincerely,

Selina Sidey. Casting Director.

Mr. Daniel Zisky,
Film & Television Copyrights,
139 Elm Park Mansions,
Park Walk,
LONDON,   SW10

15th June 1987

Dear Daniel Zisky,

Re: CRACK UP

Further to our telephone conversation this afternoon, I have
pleasure in enclosing details of the clients we discussed:-

VIRGINIA McKENNA

DON HENDERSON   The Duchess of Dorset

SHIRLEY STELFOX   Fred Smallworthy

STEPHEN GARLICK   Rita Smallworthy

MICHELE CORAL   Kevin Smallworthy

WILLIAM ABNEY   Tracey Smallworthy

RICHARD KATES   Duke of Dorset

AYNE LEIGH-COLLINS   Marquis of Beauchamp

LLY JOHNSON   Henrietta
      or
ARLOTTE SEELY   Princess Soszynski

you can get some pages over to me before Virginia goes to
ia on Wednesday, I will have them biked to her home on
nesday morning.

kindest regards,

s sincerely,

Derek Webster

WEBSTER

DON HENDERSON

JILLY JOHNSON

VIRGINIA McKENNA

Don Henderson

August 10 th. 87.

Dear Selina.

Thank you for letting me see a segment of the script of the screenplay for the forthcoming film of "Crack-up", via my personal manager, Derek Webster, of "A.i.m".

It's not often that one gets sent a section of a script of such a masterful excellence!! Quite brilliantly written, in fact!

If the entire script

of/ is as witty, and as brilliantly written, as the section you sent to me, I would be more than interested in the project, and in the possibility of playing the role of the part you have me in mind for.

Looking forward to meeting you, and the Director, in due course.

Forgive delay in contacting you personally (I told Derek Webster to pass on to you my feelings), but I have been filming overseas for a while.

Every good wish. Yours. Don.

FILM AND TELEVISION COPYRIGHTS

139 Elm Park Mansions
Park Walk
London SW10

Tel: 01 – 352 9689
Telegrams: Concept London

Mr Derek Webster
AIM
5 Denmark Street
London WC2H 8LP.

16th June 1987.

Dear Derek,

It was great talking to you on the phone today concerning the possibility of Don 'Bulmer' Henderson and Virginia 'Elsa the Lion' McKenna playing the parts respectively of Norman Smallhampton (formerly Fred Smallworthy) and the drunken Duchess of Dorset in our exciting TV series CRACK-UP.

On consideration I do not think that the role of the Duchess of Dorset as it now stands would be good enough for Miss McKenna. It has been cut considerably - indeed it has disappeared entirely - and we are thinking of offering it to Moira Lister. Admittedly, the script is being substantially re-written at the moment by Nicholas Coleridge of Harpers & Queen and if the Duchess is reinstated I'll submit draft scenes for Miss McKenna's perusal on her return from India.

I now enclose certain of Norman Smallhampton's better scenes for Don Henderson to read and very much look forward to hearing his reaction. I also enclose some other scenes in case you have other artistes available for key roles. We are particularly looking for an actor to play the part of the cabinet minister on the kebab skewer. Do you by any chance represent Barry Foster?

I very much look forward to receiving your suggestions.

Yours sincerely,

Selina Sidey

Selina Sidey. Casting Director.

PS. Since dictating the above to my secretary Julia Mortimer, I've just received your letter with other casting suggestions! I think we'd very much like to see Jilly Johnson and Charlotte Seely for the part of the nasty little tart Princess Soszynski.

Jimmy Smits ~~Milton Goldfarb~~ Alan Rachins Daniel Ziskie Aaron Seltzer Sandy McPeak ~~Jill Eikenberry~~ Jeremy Cox
~~Angela Picano~~ Max Templeton Julia Mortimer

WASA FILM PRODUCTION (UK) LIMITED

Julia Verdin
Executive Vice President

49 Park Lane
Second Floor
London W1Y 4EQ
Tel: 01-491 2822
Telex: 264833 SAFING

Miss Saidi
Film & Television Rights
139 Elm Park Mansions
Park Walk
LONDON
SW10

16th June 1987

Dear Miss Saidi

I am Head of Creative Development for Wasa Films, a U.K. based company
backed by Mr Wafic Said.

We recently produced "The Fourth Protocol" in conjunction with Rank
Films and are currently producing a mini series called "The Moon is
a Balloon" based on the David Niven Autobiography with the BBC.

I read about your project and it sounded interesting so if you are
looking for any other partners please get in touch. I am currently
looking for other projects.

Yours sincerely

JULIA VERDIN
JV/cr/FTR

Registered Office: 14 Dominion Street, London EC2M 2RJ Registered in England No: 1591281

Ms Julia Verdin
Wasa Film Production (UK) Ltd
49 Park Lane
London W1.

139 Elm Park Mansions
Park Walk
London SW10

Tel: 01 – 352 9689
Telegrams: Concept London

17th June 1987.

Dear Miss Verdin,

You may well be looking for projects, madam, but we're not looking for outside finance.

CRACK-UP is fully backed by my uncle on my mother's side, Mr Joe Columbo of Gambino, Ziskie, Columbo & Seltzer inc (Clean Towels and Pizzas) of New York.

Should you be looking for finance for 'The Moon's A Balloon' by all means let me know and I will approach my uncle. I cannot hold out much hope, however, since I happen to know that he always found Niven to be a most unpleasant man.

Yours sincerely,

Selina Sidey.

Selina Sidey. Creative Development and Finance Director.

FILM AND TELEVISION COPYRIGHTS

Laurence Evans Esq
ICM Ltd
388 Oxford Street
London W1N 9HE.

139 Elm Park Mansions
Park Walk
London SW10

Tel: 01 – 352 9689
Telegrams: Concept London

16th June 1987.

Dear Mr Evans,

Hi! I'm the new Casting Director on CRACK-UP and I have to tell you that I have had no reply as yet to my letter of 9th June to your Miss Vacca. I hope this doesn't mean that Sir John Gielgud is no longer interested in playing the part of the barmy Duke of Dorset in the series. I now enclose his best scene - his only scene, in fact' - confident that after he has read it he will be with us 200%.

The really brilliant news is that we are making our first press announcement next week in the form of an exclusive interview with Baz 'The Man Who Knows The Stars' Bigbamboye of The Daily Mail. Could you confirm as soon as possible that it will be okay for Sandy McPeak (our PR Director) to announce Sir John's involvement?

I believe you also represent Sir Rex Harrison. Would he be available to play the part of Prime Minister Macmillan in a small but important scene? Perhaps you could let me know this when giving us the go-ahead to announce Sir John's involvement.

With best wishes,

Yours sincerely,

Selina Sidey.

Selina Sidey. Casting Director.

Enc. CRACK-UP, Episode 8, Scene 2.

CRACK-UP. Episode 8. Scene 2. INTERIOR. JUDGE HENRY HERBERT QC's room at Knightsbridge Crown Court. JUDGE HERBERT QC, a distinguished silver-haired man in his late fifties is reading some papers at his desk. There is a knock on the door.

JUDGE HERBERT QC: Come!

(Enter his clerk, EDWARD).

EDWARD: You have some visitors, your Honour.

JUDGE HERBERT QC (glancing at his watch): At this hour? Who can they be?

EDWARD: Mr. Robert Sampson QC, your Honour, who is defending that disgusting young man the Marquis of Beauchamp, and his father, the half-mad Duke of Dorset.

RICHARD WEST: The real madmen, of course, are not the patients in top security hospitals but the psychiatrists who let them loose to kill again.

PEREGRINE WORSTHORNE: I wish I could believe that the long-term Broadmoor prisoner would be <u>less</u> of a danger to the general public rather than more as a result of studying sociology at the Open University.

JUDGE HERBERT QC: Thank you, Edward. Show them in.

(HERBERT rises to greet his visitors. Enter ROBERT SAMPSON QC and THE DUKE OF DORSET, a stricken, weak-faced man in his early sixties).

SAMPSON: Morning Henry. May I introduce the Duke of Dorset?

DORSET: Where am I? Who am I? Oh my God!

SAMPSON: Take it easy, old fellow. You're in good hands.

JUDGE HERBERT QC: How do you do?

DORSET: Call me Boofy. Oh my God! My poor boy!

SAMPSON: Steady there, Boofy.

JUDGE HERBERT QC: Won't you sit down? Care for a sherry?

SAMPSON: Bit early for me, thank you, Henry.

RICHARD WEST: I'll have a yard of real ale, thank you very much. What was good enough for old Jack Falstaff is good enough for me.

JUDGE HERBERT QC: Boofy?

(DORSET doesn't reply. He buries his head in his hands and mumbles to himself).

JUDGE HERBERT QC: Tragic. Absolutely tragic.

GEOFFREY WHEATCROFT: Surely it was that wise and agreeable man John Mortimer who pointed out that anyone could write a tragedy but that writing a comedy requires real skill?

RICHARD WEST: How true! No doubt Bill Shakespeare laboured for many months over The Merry Wives of Windsor but tossed off Lear in a weekend.

JUDGE HERBERT QC: So, what can I do for you, Robert?

SAMPSON: Frankly, Henry, I was wondering what you thought of my plea? The case against young Beauchamp is rotten actually.

DORSET: My poor boy! I blame myself! It wasn't his mother's fault!

SAMPSON: That's reasonable.

IRMA KURTZ: Male reasonableness is a form of rape.

ANNA RAEBURN: Men invented language and use it to suppress women.

CHRISTOPHER BOOKER: This is the wooly-minded jargon of militant feminists!

MAX HASTINGS: Would that Orwell were with us now!

GEOFFREY WHEATCROFT: What a shame Dr Leavis never learned to write agreeable English!

JUDGE HERBERT QC: You're referring to the supplying charge, I take it, Robert?

SAMPSON: Of course. Where's the evidence for it, Henry?

JUDGE HERBERT QC (consulting his papers): I see he bought £25,000 worth of cocaine in a month. That's a lot of cocaine, Robert.

SAMPSON: For his own use, Henry. He never dealt. What evidence is there that he dealt?

JUDGE HERBERT QC: None at all, I'll grant you that. It's my view that the boy fell in with a bad lot.

DORSET: He did! He did! Money men! Brokers! Men with Filofax and American mistresses!

MAX HASTINGS: Americans have no sense of irony, of course.

SAMPSON: I was referring more to the friends he made after hours, Boofy. Greeks, black men, women of Polish birth.

JUDGE HERBERT QC: I don't like the look of them at all, I don't like the cut of their jibs in the least. The black man will get eight years, I tell you frankly, Robert. And the Greek's no better. He'll get five.

SAMPSON: And so they should, Henry. They took my client down a dark and tangled path. Led him every step of the way.

JUDGE HERBERT QC: What about the woman? The Polish woman? This Soszynski creature? Your client's - er - quick wash before dinner, was she? Excuse the Anglo-Saxon.

DORSET: God forbid! A Polish woman!

SAMPSON: I think not, Henry. But about my client. What's your verdict, then?

JUDGE HERBERT QC: Hm - all right, I'll support your plea. I'll dismiss the supplying charge when we return to court.

DORSET: Thank God! Thank God! I'll have that sherry now.

JUDGE HERBERT QC: There's still the possession charge. The boy's got a bad record, Robert. I can't let him go Scot free.

SAMPSON: You're not thinking of a custodial sentence, are you, Henry? What purpose would that serve? The boy's a pathetic - excuse me, Boofy - a pathetic wreck of a human being. What good would a prison sentence serve?

JUDGE HERBERT QC: Inclined to agree, Robert. In a clinic, is he?

SAMPSON: Indeed. And making good progress.

JUDGE HERBERT QC: You'll plead guilty to the possession charge?

DORSET (Leaping to his feet in horror): Oh my God! You're on a possession charge, Robert? How did this happen? We must get you the best legal advice that money can buy! Oh my God!

SAMPSON: Not me, you...you...stupid old.....sorry. No, Alexander. Your son. We're talking about your son here, Boofy.

DORSET: Thank God. I'd no idea you used.

SAMPSON: If I plead to the possession charge, Henry, will you waive the custodial sentence?

JUDGE HERBERT QC: I'm sympathetic to the idea, Robert. Can't see it would do the boy much good to lock the boy up. Do the black fellow a bit of good, of course.

SAMPSON: And the Greek.

JUDGE HERBERT QC: Yes, and the Greek. Don't like the look of him at all. The Polish woman's all right, though.

SAMPSON: Led astray, I dare say, like my client. What will it be, then, Henry? Probation?

JUDGE HERBERT QC: Can't be probation. He's on probation already.

SAMPSON: Well I never! So he is. You had me there and no mistake!

JUDGE HERBERT QC: One year suspended for two? What would you say to that?

SAMPSON: That's fair, Henry, that's very fair.

JUDGE HERBERT QC: All right. It's agreed. We'd better go back into court. I'll dismiss the supplying charge and the rest's agreed. Let's get on with it.

(Exit JUDGE HERBERT, ROBERT SAMPSON QC and THE DUKE OF DORSET).

BERNARD LEVIN: To lawyers, of course, a brief is just a piece of paper with a price tag on it.

FADE.

ICM

INTERNATIONAL CREATIVE MANAGEMENT, LTD.

Miss Selina Sidey,
Casting Director,
Film & Television Copyrights,
139 Elm Park Mansions,
Park Walk,
London SW10.

17th June 1987.

Dear Miss Sidey,

<u>Sir John Gielgud</u>

I refer to the letters from your Company dated June 3rd, 5th and 16th.

Please be advised that at no time have we indicated that Sir John Gielgud has any interest in being involved in your project "Crack-Up".

It would, therefore, be totally incorrect for you to refer to Sir John in any interview with Mr. Baz Bamigboye of the Daily Mail.

We do also represent Mr. Rex Harrison, but he will not be available for the role of Prime Minister Macmillan in your series.

Yours sincerely,

Laurence Evans

Laurence Evans

cc: Julia Mortimer
Jeremy Cox

2nd Floor.
68, Old Brompton Road, London, SW7 3LQ.

Telephone: 01-581 2478

DIRECTORS:
PETER T. CHARLESWORTH
PRISCILLA BERGUS (U.S.A.)

June 17, 1987

Ms. Julia Mortimer
Film and Television Copyrights
139 Elm Park Mansions
Park Walk
London SW10

Dear Ms. Mortimer,

CRACK-UP

I would be grateful if you would consider the following suggestions for the above named production.

ACTOR	PART
NORMAN ROSSINGTON	Fred Smallworthy
LONNIE DONEGAN	"
PHILIP GOODHEW	the Marquis of Beauchamp
LEWIS JONES	Lord Denning
VALERIE WALSH	Rita Smallworthy
TATTIANA COLOMBO	Henrietta
MANDY PERRYMENT	Mandy Rice-Davies

I enclose the relevant CVs and photographs and hope these ideas prove useful to you.

Yours sincerely,

Priscilla Berg

NORMAN ROSSINGTON

LONNIE DONEGAN

MANDY PERRYMEN

FILM AND TELEVISION COPYRIGHTS

139 Elm Park Mansions
Park Walk
London SW10

Tel: 01 – 352 9689
Telegrams: Concept London

Miss Priscilla Bergus (USA)
Peter Charlesworth Ltd
68 Old Brompton Road
London, SW7.

19th June 1987.

Dear Priscilla,

Many thanks for your letter of 17th June, which I am replying to on behalf of my assistant Julia Mortimer.

I'm afraid I've never heard of Norman Rossington or Lonnie Donegan, but I have one of those funny, tickly 'casting hunches' that Mandy Perryment might be exactly right for the part of Mandy Rice-Davies. She looks really cute! Cute, of course, is the last thing you'd call Mandy Rice-Davies now, but I suppose she must have been okay back in 1953 or whenever it was, otherwise all those silly old men wouldn't have fallen for her! Men! Anyway – if your Mandy would like to see some scenes in which she'd be involved, let me know soonest and I'll get them over to her. Then, perhaps, she'd like to meet our Director, Lindsey Anderson. When she does, I suggest she wears as few clothes as possible, as I expect he's a typical man!

Hey – I see you're from the States! You must know the Family – my Uncle Joe, my Aunt Maria and my cousin Joe Jr who's been running the Family, of course, since Uncle Joe's accident. We must get together for a good natter some time.

I look forward to hearing from you.

Yours,

Selina Sidey. Casting Director.

JOSEPH AND WAGG

SECOND FLOOR : 78, NEW BOND STREET : LONDON: W1Y 9DA : TEL. 01-629 1048/9

Theatre, films and television

Ms Julia Mortimer,
c/o Film and TV Copyrights,
139, Elm Park Mansions,
Park Walk,
LONDON SW10.

18th June 1987

Dear Julia,

Re: **CRACK-UP**

I understand that you are currently looking to cast the above mentioned drama/documentary and I would like to make the following suggestions:-

	DEIRDRE COSTELLO	Sp. No. 223
	JANINE WOOD	Sp. No. 2459
Rita Smallworthy		Sp. No. 2939
Tracey Smallworthy	ADAM NORTON	Sp. No. 3126
The Marquis of Beauchamp	ADAM TOMLINSON	Sp. No. 2274
	CATHERINE RABETT	Sp. No. 1370
Henrietta	THERESE LIOTARD	
Princess Soszynski	WILLIAM WILDE	
Lord Lambton		

I hope that these ideas will prove to be of use. I have enclosed photographs and CVs where possible, but unfortunately we do not have any photographs of **WILLIAM WILDE** and neither is he in Spotlight, but if you would like to meet him or any other clients please do not hesitate to contact me.

I look forward to hearing from you.

Best wishes.

Yours sincerely,

JANE LEHRER

ANY OFFER CONTAINED IN THIS LETTER DOES N...
LICENSED BY THE SECRETARY OF STATE FOR EMPLOYMENT UNDER THE EMP...

E. M. Joseph

CATHERINE RABETT

10 June 1987

Daniel Ziskie,
Executive Producer
Film and Television Copyrights
139 Elm Park Mansions
Park Walk
London SW10

Dear Mr Ziskie,

Thank you for your letter and I am glad you liked my article in the
Sunday Telegraph. Your TV series sounds rather interesting. I
would not be able to help you in any way that kept me out of this
office but I would be more than happy to look at the script and
screen it for inaccuracies.

Do let me know what the understanding is that you propose.

With my best regards,

_____
Nicholas Coleridge
Editor

FILM AND TELEVISION COPYRIGHTS

139 Elm Park Mansions
Park Walk
London SW10

Tel: 01 – 352 9689
Telegrams: Concept London

Nicholas Coleridge Esq
Harpers & Queen
72 Broadwick Street
London W1V 2BP.

17th June 1987.

Dear Mr Coleridge,

Thank you for your letter of 10th June. We're all delighted here that you are available and keen to do a quick re-write job on CRACK-UP.

I now enclose some draft scenes and would ask you to have a close look at those involving the Marquis of Beauchamp and his father the barmy Duke of Dorset. These particularly seem to fall within your area of expertise – the correct way currently to peel a kumquat, the au courant lie of the turn-up etc plus authentic 'Powder Room' exchanges.

Should I discuss money with your agent? I imagine we would pay you the standard rate for a re-write job. Perhaps you could let me know whether you've done this sort of thing before.

Yours sincerely,

Daniel Ziskie. Producer.

Enc. CRACK-UP, Episode 1, Scene 8, Episode 5, Scene 7, Episode 6, Scene 8, Episode 7, Scene 2.

CRACK-UP. Episode 1. Scene 8. INTERIOR. The gentleman's lavatory at Morgan, Carey, Collier & Co, a City Merchant Bank and Overnight Money House. Present: BANKERS, BROKERS, JOBBERS, KEVIN SMALLHAMPTON and the MARQUIS OF BEAUCHAMP, a cherry-lipped aristocrat in his late twenties. Time: 8 am.

1st BANKER: Damn me. Drew a duff kumquat last night. Feel a bit dicky actually.

2nd BANKER: Excuse me. Got to gross up. Senior hangover.

3rd BANKER: Bead and breakfast?

1st BANKER: Hospital tackle. I'm back to back with Ernest Saunders.

4th BANKER: Tactical pay-outs?

1st BANKER: Jobbing backwards. Excuse me.

1st COMMODITY BROKER: I'm four-walling.

2nd COMMODITY BROKER: So you are. Revolving credit?

1st COMMODITY BROKER: A dawn raid. Over-night money.

GEOFFREY WHEATCROFT: The essence of money, of course, is that it has no value. Surely it was that agreeable man Carlyle who said: 'Whoso has sixpence is sovereign - to the length of a sixpence - over all men; commands cooks to feed him, philosophers to teach him, kings to mount guard over him - to the length of a sixpence'.

3rd COMMODITY BROKER: Bone me up the arse will you, old chappie, ta.

1st BANKER: Space-cake?

2nd BANKER: Dead cat bounce.

3rd BANKER: Watch out everyone! Here comes Sir Peter Carey!

(Enter SIR PETER CAREY - a hard nut.)

SIR PETER CAREY: You're all fired!

BANKERS, BROKERS, etc: Oh hell! What a downer eh ya!

SIR PETER CAREY (standing next to KEVIN SMALLHAMPTON at the urinal): Name?

KEVIN: Smallhampton, sir.

SIR PETER CAREY: How dare you!

KEVIN: That's my name, sir.

SIR PETER CAREY: Well done.

(SIR PETER CAREY exits).

THE MARQUIS OF BEAUCHAMP (to KEVIN): Hullo there. Your first day is it?

KEVIN: Oh. Er. Yes. Thank you. Sorry.

THE MARQUIS OF BEAUCHAMP: Mine too. Bit of a drag what?

1st BANKER: No thanks Beauchamp. Too early for me actually.
Drew this duff kumquat do you see?

KEVIN: There's a lot to learn.

THE MARQUIS OF BEAUCHAMP: Ambitious little tick are you?

KEVIN: I suppose so. I don't want to let my father down. It
was three-to-the-shirt where he was born and the outside bucket.
I want to be a credit to him.

THE MARQUIS OF BEAUCHAMP: That's a laugh! Mine's a proper drag.

1st BANKER: Still too early. Thanks all the same.

2nd COMMODITY BROKER: I'm wanted on the other line.

THE MARQUIS OF BEAUCHAMP: Okay ya. That's a senior idea.
(To KEVIN). Care for a line?

KEVIN: Pardon? Sorry? What?

THE MARQUIS OF BEAUCHAMP: A line. A toot. A snort. Up the nose.

KEVIN: Oh. I don't think so. Thank you awfully.

THE MARQUIS OF BEAUCHAMP: Please yourself. I'm going to.

(BEAUCHAMP produces a little white envelope, lays out a line of
coke and takes it up the nose.)

THE MARQUIS OF BEAUCHAMP: Here not bad I say! Goodness wow.
Quite a bell-ringer actually. Better cooked of course. You
every cooked it Smallhampton?

KEVIN: I don't believe I have.

THE MARQUIS OF BEAUCHAMP: Good heavens! You are a naive little
tick!

KEVIN: I suppose I am. Sorry.

THE MARQUIS OF BEAUCHAMP: We'll soon change that. What are you
doing tonight?

KEVIN: Oh. I thought I'd study. Take some work home. I mustn't
let my father down.

THE MARQUIS OF BEAUCHAMP: Ha! What else are fathers for? Come
to a party. Why not. At Princess Soszynski's. She's a senior
tart do you see? You'll like her I say. Care to come?

KEVIN: Well I don't know really. I ought to work.

THE MARQUIS OF BEAUCHAMP: Oh pah! Come to the party! Why not
I say.

KEVIN: Okay, yes, all right, I suppose so. I mean thank you
very much. That's jolly decent of you Beauchamp.

THE MARQUIS OF BEAUCHAMP: Call me Alexander. Top hole. I'll
pick you up later in my Porsche and we'll zap over there together.

Where do you live?

KEVIN: 44 Acton Avenue.

THE MARQUIS OF BEAUCHAMP: Good God. On second thoughts - I'll meet you at Soszynski's. Flat 7, Bristol House, Lower Sloane Street. About ten o'clock. Okay?

KEVIN: Thanks awfully Beauchamp.

MAX HASTINGS: They're on a slippery slope.

FADE.

CRACK-UP. Episode 5. Scene 7. INTERIOR. Flat 7, Bristol House, Lower Sloane Street, London SW3, the home of PRINCESS SOSZYNSKI, a self-employed Polish woman, a woman easily ignited in the early afternoon. Present: PRINCESS SOSZYNSKI, THE MARQUIS OF BEAUCHAMP, GREEK GEORGE (a dwarf), ZAPHYRE (a black man in a pork-pie hat), GIRLS FROM THE THAI EMBASSY, GIRLS CALLED MANDY, CANDY, LINDY, CINDY, etc, GOSSIP COLUMNISTS, BROKERS, BANKERS, BOGGLERS, BONKERS, BIMBOS, OLD HARROVIANS, BLACK GIRLS, LESBIANS - all of whom have been corrupted by the venomously beautiful, leather-clad sadist PRINCESS SOSZYNSKI and her slave, the grovelling, cherry-lipped MARQUIS OF BEAUCHAMP. They are all free-basing, smoking cocaine in a glass pipe. There are long silences, followed by unintelligible attempts at conversation. There is much unnecessary nudity. Occasionally a couple grapple clumsily but they have lost so much weight that their bones scrape together with a noise like Janet Street-Porter drawing her front-teeth down a blackboard. The worst affected crawl on the floor, licking the carpet for remnants of oil. Some sob and bite each other's shoes. Others fondle the pipe, examining its ducts and gulleys for bits to lick.

PRINCESS SOSZYNSKI: Wow!

THE MARQUIS OF BEAUCHAMP: Wow! Oh Christ!

GREEK GEORGE: Yeah! All right.

GIRL FROM THE THAI EMBASSY: Wow!

MANDY, CANDY, LINDY, CINDY, etc: Wow!

LESBIANS, BLACK GIRLS, BIMBOS, BROKERS: Fucking hell!

(There is a knock on the door. Eventually someone crawls over to answer it. Enter KEVIN SMALLHAMPTON, looking very nervous.)

KEVIN: Hullo.

THE MARQUIS OF BEAUCHAMP: Yeah. Wow.

KEVIN (uncertainly): Yeah wow.

THE MARQUIS OF BEAUCHAMP: What time is it anyone?

PRINCESS SOSZYNSKI: Who cares?

GREEK GEORGE: Too right! What day is it?

ALL: Yeah! What day is it!

(PRINCESS SOSZYNSKI takes off all her clothes. She looks as tempting as a poisoned nectarine).

PRINCESS SOSZYNSKI: Blowback, anyone?

BLACK GIRL: Yeah wow!

(PRINCESS SOSZYNSKI and BLACK GIRL perform the ritual of blow-back, one drawing deeply on the pipe and then blowing the smoke directly into the other's lungs. The BLACK GIRL'S eyes start

from her head like grapes on a pin. She clutches her chest,
falls over backwards and lies on the carpet in a coma, her heels
drumming on the floor.)

PRINCESS SOSZYNSKI: Wow! That worked!

THE MARQUIS OF BEAUCHAMP: God I feel randy actually. I'm on
fire here I tell you. Tear off all my clothes and cover me
with marmite! Do whatever you like with me I say! What about
you, Soszynski? How would you like to make £17.50 the hard way?

PRINCESS SOSZYNSKI: Cash?

THE MARQUIS OF BEAUCHAMP: A cheque actually.

PRINCESS SOSZYNSKI: What! Your last three bounced!

THE MARQUIS OF BEAUCHAMP: I'm broke actually. Daddy won't
cough up. (He turns to KEVIN SMALLHAMPTON, who is sitting
nervously in a corner). Look here, Smallhampton, lend me
£17.50 I say.

KEVIN: Of course Beau - er - Alexander.

(KEVIN takes out his wallet and opens it. BEAUCHAMP snatches
the wallet, peels off £17, which he hands to SOSZYNSKI, then
puts the wallet in his pocket.)

THE MARQUIS OF BEAUCHAMP: Thanks Smallhampton.

(PRINCESS SOSZYNSKI puts the money in her Louis Vuitton Departure
Lounge handbag, then absent-mindedly pins BEAUCHAMP to the carpet.
Everyone looks away in disgust.)

MARY KENNY: Promiscuous people are essentially lonely, searching
angrily for love. This is a cry for help.

MALCOLM MUGGERIDGE: They say that Casanova, the Florentine
womaniser, once slept with eight different women in one night.

MICHAEL PARKINSON: That can't be bad!

MALCOLM MUGGERIDGE: He was homosexual, no doubt, and probably
impotent.

MICHAEL PARKINSON: That can't be good!

KEVIN SMALLHAMPTON: Oh my God! What's to become of me?

RICHARD WEST: He's on the M1 to nowhere.

(Enter NORMAN SMALLHAMPTON, head-first through the front-door,
splintering it into a thousand pieces. He is foaming with rage
like a fighting bull.)

NORMAN SMALLHAMPTON: I'll tell you what's to become of you,
boy! You'll get a whacking and then I'm dragging you out of this
hell-hole!

KEVIN SMALLHAMPTON: Oh my goodness. My father's going to box me
to the floor.

(NORMAN SMALLHAMPTON whacks his son, then king-punches THE MARQUIS
OF BEAUCHAMP, GREEK GEORGE, BROKERS, BANKERS, GOSSIP COLUMNISTS
and the BLACK GIRL, knocking them all cold.)

FADE.

CRACK-UP. Episode 6. Scene 8. INTERIOR. PRINCESS SOSZYNSKI'S flat, 7 Bristol House, Lower Sloane Street, London SW3. Present: PRINCESS SOSZYNSKI, GREEK GEORGE, GIRLS FROM THE THAI EMBASSY, GIRLS CALLED MANDY, CANDY, LINDY, CINDY, etc, GOSSIP COLUMNISTS, BANKERS, BIMBOS, OLD HARROVIANS, BLACK GIRLS and KEVIN SMALLHAMPTON, who has lost three stone in weight but is looking much less ill-at-ease. They are all free-basing. Late evening.

KEVIN: Oh wow!

PRINCESS SOSZYNSKI: Yeah! Wow.

GREEK GEORGE: Yeah. All right!

MANDY, CANDY, LINDY, CINDY, etc: Yeah wow.

KEVIN (putting his arm round PRINCESS SOSZYNSKI): Blow-back?

PRINCESS SOSZYNSKI: Yeah. Sure.

(They perform the ritual of blow-back. They fall over backwards, their heels drumming on the carpet. PRINCESS SOSZYNSKI comes to first).

PRINCESS SOSZYNSKI: Wow. You're cute. I'd rather have your father though. Wow! What a man!

KEVIN: Ha! My father's a real drag! I've let him down, but I don't care!

(Suddenly the front door comes down off its hinges with a terrible splintering noise.)

KEVIN: Oh goodness. Here he comes again.

BLACK GIRL: Probably my mother. Wanting to know why I haven't written.

MANDY, CANDY, LINDY, CINDY, etc: Mothers!

PRINCESS SOSZYNSKI: Yeah mothers. Still, you should keep in touch.

(Enter a team of Drug Squad officers led by DETECTIVE SERGEANT JONES).

D/S JONES: Evening all. We're the filth. This is a top society bust. Oh dear me! The evil Marquis of Beauchamp doesn't seem to be here. How infuriating.

GREEK GEORGE (putting his hands up): He's at the dungeon.

D/S JONES: Are you referring to the basement flat underneath A & S Menswear in the Edgeware Road, run by Angelos Savvides, the fat Cypriot?

ALL (except KEVIN): That's right. He's there now with fat Angelos.

KEVIN: You unpardonable sneaks I say!

D/S JONES: Who are you?

KEVIN: Smallhampton, Sergeant.

D/S JONES: I can see that. Put some clothes on. Right -
you're all under arrest.

ALL: It's not our fault. We're sick. We need help.

A FISHY CHRISTIAN COUNSELLOR FROM BROADWAY LODGE (a drug
addiction clinic practising the sinister Minnesota Method):
Of course you do. That will be £800 per week plus VAT for a
six week course of group therapy. Defecating into a bucket on
an open podium in front of a roomful of emotional cripples.
Cure by humiliation - the Christian way. Two weeks in advance.
Sign here.

FADE.

CRACK-UP. Episode 7. Scene 2. EXTERIOR. Beauchamp Palace, the stately seat of the DUKE OF DORSET. Early PM. NORMAN SMALLHAMPTON is striding purposefully up the long drive, scattering lions, tourists and Americans with his stick. He rings loudly at the great front-door. ARCHIBALD, a stooped retainer, opens it.

ARCHIBALD: Circus folk round the back.

(He slams the door in SMALLHAMPTON'S face.)

CHRISTOPHER BOOKER: Mention of circuses, I imagine, will elicit from wooly-minded do-gooders the usual parrot-cry of 'Cruelty to animals!'

MARY KENNY: Our children are being robbed of their childhood.

(SMALLHAMPTON, in a fury, bangs on the door with his fist. ARCHIBALD eventually re-opens it.)

ARCHIBALD: Round the back, I said.

SMALLHAMPTON (taking ARCHIBALD by the throat and lifting him off his feet): Look you monkey, less of round the back, if you don't mind, and escort me pronto to his lordship.

ARCHIBALD: Urgle, urgle.

(SMALLHAMPTON releases ARCHIBALD, who collapses in a heap, holding his throat).

THE DUKE OF DORSET (calling out from the drawing-room): What is it actually? What's cooking Archibald I say.

ARCHIBALD: Urgle. Urgle.

(SMALLHAMPTON steps over ARCHIBALD'S body and enters the palace. He finds his way to the drawing-room, where the DUKE OF DORSET is feeding a lettuce to his goat. THE DUCHESS OF DORSET is lying on a chaise-longue, an empty bottle of gin by her side.)

SMALLHAMPTON: Your grace! (He bows). Pardon my breath, it was eggs for tea.

DUKE OF DORSET: Call me Boofy. Have we met? What? Jog my memory. Memory not what it was. Nothing is, come to that.

SMALLHAMPTON: Never had the honour, Boofy, but our two lads know each other.

DUKE OF DORSET: Good God what next?

SMALLHAMPTON: Arrested cheek by jowl in fact.

DUKE OF DORSET: Goats and monkeys! Arrested you say? My boy? With yours? Good grief! How sad!

SMALLHAMPTON: Surely you knew?

DUKE OF DORSET: Lot on my mind. Devilishly difficult to heat, these old houses. Your house, Littlejohn.....

SMALLHAMPTON: Smallhampton.

DUKE OF DORSET: Really? How sad. Anyway, your house, Littlejohn, how do you heat it? Tell me that I say.

SMALLHAMPTON: I don't have a house, Boofy, just a duplex with lounge-diner at the better end of Acton Avenue. About your boy.....

DUKE OF DORSET: In trouble is he? Don't remember that. A thousand pounds a week it costs to heat this place.....

SMALLHAMPTON: We must <u>do</u> something, Boofy.

DUKE OF DORSET: Yes, but what? I can't move. Got to keep the old place on.....

SMALLHAMPTON: About our <u>lads</u>, Boofy, not your fucking heating bill! Pardon my French. Spoke as we found where I came from. It was three to the shirt and the outside bucket.

THE DUKE OF DORSET: Oh.

THE DUCHESS OF DORSET (falling off her chaise-longue and struggling to her feet): I'd better prepare dinner. (EXITS).

GEOFFREY WHEATCROFT: Apartheid's most uncongenial aspect, perhaps, is that it breeds habits of indolence. In Great Britain the ruling classes can at least cook a tolerable meal for themselves and their guests. In South Africa, on the other hand, one of the most dis-agreeable consequences of living in a serf society is demonstrated by the fact that the rich eat filthy food cooked by their coloured servants!

SMALLHAMPTON: I plan to form Fathers Anonymous, that's what. To fight drugs and corruption in the City. A vigilante group of fathers. Are you in, Boofy?

DUKE OF DORSET: Can you do anything about heating this damn place?

(SMALLHAMPTON, seeing that the DUKE OF DORSET is a broken man, leaves abruptly, tapping ARCHIBALD to the ground as he exits).

SMALLHAMPTON (striding back down the long drive): Damn it, I'll do it on my own! I'll form Fathers Anonymous! I'll move mountains! I'll see the Prime Minister herself! She's a father! She'll understand!

FADE.

Jeffrey Archer
Alembic House
93 Albert Embank...
London SE1.

Handwritten note on Harpers & Queen letterhead:

25 June 87

Dear Mr Ziskel

Thank you for your letter and script. I intend to look at it this weekend, and will give you my detailed views on the dialogue & Beauchamp and Dorset.

I will put my agent Lesley Gardner to contact to safely you.

Yours Sincerely

Niamh Coleridge

Harpers & Queen · National Magazine House · 72 Broadwick Street, London W1V 2BP ☎ 01-439 7144

---

352 9689
grams: Concept Lond...

22nd June 1987.

Dear Mr Archer,

Many thanks indeed for your letter of 11th June, and I quite understand that you would like to keep the news of your involvement in CRACK-UP under wraps for a while. I hope that in spite of this you were as pleased as we were by the advance publicity we received last week in Today and The Sunday Times (copies enclosed in case your cuttings service hasn't sent them yet.)

I do see why you can't comment on the Monica Coghlin affair at the moment but could you at least answer my queries about your involvement, or otherwise, in the earlier scandals mentioned in my last letter? The Profumo, Lambton and Janie Jones affairs are not still sub judice, as far as I know. (Incidentally, if you're looking for a really hot solicitor, can I recommend Theodore Goddard? They did a really great job for my friend Jamie Blandford last year and he was up on a cracking awful charge. Poor Jamie - he hasn't had a lot of luck, I'm afraid.)

Sandy McPeak, our PR Director, has meanwhile asked me to enclose with this letter one of our standard PR forms which he would like you to fill in and return. We won't be sending it out at the moment, but will keep it on file until we go into production. Oh - and Sandy says how great it is to be dealing with someone who really under-stands PR. You've certainly bumped this business with the Irish tart into a big one! Sandy says it will run and run!

I look forward to hearing from you.

Yours,

Selina Sidey. Casting Director.

Encs. 'Today' and 'The Sunday Times'.

...int, an expanded section dedicated to
Screen & Print will provide unrivalled
...g and film industries

Sally Soames

Nation in the dock

THE moral standards of Britain's best and brightest are to be chronicled in an extraordinary 10-hour, £10m drama documentary television serial in which actors will play, among many others, Cecil Parkinson, Sara Keays, Jeffrey Archer and John Profumo.

The serial, Crack-Up, will feature two fictional families – that of the mad Lord Dorset and his corrupt offspring, the other the Smallworthys, a humble family whose son goes into the City and is led astray by the Dorset's drug- and drink-crazed heir. Interwoven with that will be contemporary newsreel footage and interviews with genuine figures of controversy, carried out by the fictional Smallworthy Sr.

In the casting notes, Crack-Up's executive producer, Daniel Ziskie, says the project will "trace the moral decline of this country over the past 25 years, drawing a connection between the Swinging Sixties (Lady Chatterley, the mini-skirt, the pill, Rachmanism, Christine Keeler, Roy Jenkins' unhappy performance at the Foreign Office, Ready Steady Go, etc.) and today's squalid scandals in the City and in the Tory party (insider dealings, 'unusual payments', teenage commodity millionaires on so-called 'crack', shredding machines, multiple share applications by Tory MPs using aliases)."

Ziskie says he has encountered no real opposition from the celebrities who will come under the serial's baleful gaze. "We have approached most of the people either featured or mentioned – some of whom would appear as themselves, and some played by actors. A few refused to be interviewed, and while it would be wrong of me to say the rest were all deliriously happy, I think they understand that we won't attribute qualities or quotes to them which aren't already public knowledge."

Patrick Stoddart

Would you like to be in our sex film?

Jeffrey Archer

Fiona Wright

Sara Keays

Mary Whitehouse

Scandals on TV

THE BISHOP of London, Stock Exchange chief Sir Nicholas Goodison and Tory Jeffrey Archer have been asked to take part in a shocking new £10 million TV series, laced with full-frontal nudity and drug-crazed orgies among the aristocracy.

The series, Crack Up, dramatises famous sex scandals to satirise the notion that Britain has been plunged into moral decline because of liberal ideals unleashed in the 1960s.

Actors will play real life characters, including those involved in the Profumo affair and the Lord Lambton scandal.

Channel 4 is believed to be interested in screening the 10-part black comedy, to be made by an independent company.

Producer Daniel Ziskie yesterday confirmed that some people would either be playing themselves or giving their backing to the project.

"Jeffrey Archer said he was interested in taking part.

"Nicholas Goodison wants to refute allegations of widespread drugtaking in the City and the Bishop, Graham Leonard, shares the view that the swinging Sixties weren't responsible for liberalisation of morals."

But not everybody is backing the project. Ziskie revealed that other figures such as Sara Keays, Cecil Parkinson and Mary Whitehouse would not be giving it their blessing.

"Mary Whitehouse turned us down flat and we thought it was too sensitive a time to approach Cecil Parkinson,"

by PAULINE WALLIN

says Ziskie. And former Master of the Rolls Lord Denning yesterday hit out at the inclusion of his name in the cast list as "a silly old man, quite out of his depth in the swinging Sixties".

Lord Denning, who headed an inquiry into security after the Profumo affair, warned: "I strongly object to being described in this way."

Other casting details are equally unflattering:

● Cecil Parkinson: "An adulterer, attractive but lightweight."

● Sara Keays: "A bitter, unattractive single mother."

● John Profumo: "Weak-willed and over-sexed."

● Sir Ralph Halpern: "Rich, over-sexed tycoon."

● Fiona Wright: "Attractive in a rather common sort of way." Scenes in the series include full-frontal, nude orgies at the flat of drug addict the Marquis of Beauchamp, a fictional character. But Ziskie says: "The IBA have seen the scripts and haven't objected."

Royal romances start baby boom

by JIM GLEESON

ROYAL Family fever works better than any aphrodisiac, say doctors in Scotland.

They reached their verdict after a record number of births in Aberdeen last month. One weekend midwives delivered 47 babies within 48 hours.

At first they could not explain the baby boom. The most obvious an...

last July. Further checks showed that there was a sudden surge in the number of births nine months after the engagement of the Prince and Princess of Wales in 1981.

There was another nine months after their marriage — and two more after both Prince William and Prince Harry were born.

One doctor said...

rounding royalty could make women crave another baby and they can get very excited at births and marriages involving members of the Royal Family.

A Grampian Health Board spokesman said: "The birth rate in May broke all records."

Ironically, Fergie h...

MODERN M...

FILM AND TELEVISION COPYRIGHTS

139 Elm Park Mansions
Park Walk
London SW10

Tel: 01 – 352 9689
Telegrams: Concept London

Sir Laurence Evans
ICM Ltd
388/396 Oxford Street
London W1N 9HE.

22nd June 1987.

Dear Sir Laurence,

Many thanks for your letter of 17th June concerning Sir John Gielgud's appearance in CRACK-UP.

I take your word for it that Sir John is not 100% committed to us at the moment, but I hope the enclosed press cuttings will show him what an important series it is and persuade him to change his mind. 'NATION IN THE DOCK!' - okay!

Our Publicity Director, Sandy McPeak, had already given the news of Sir John's involvement to Mr Baz Bamigboye of the Daily Mail by the time we got your letter, so it is too late to stop the story breaking. Meanwhile, Sandy has asked me to cut a few corners by enclosing with this letter one of our standard PR forms which he would be very grateful if Sir John could fill in and return. It's quite straightforward - previous experience, favourite roles, hobbies, useful contacts, is Sir John his real name? - that sort of thing. It might have the effect of avoiding confusions in the future, Sandy thinks.

One last thing - would you please confirm that you did actually send the script we sent you to Sir John? I've been in this business long enough to know that some agents are in the habit of rejecting offers on behalf of clients without the client ever knowing about it.

I look forward to hearing from you.

Yours sincerely,

Selina Sidey.

cc.   Sir John Gielgud, South Pavilion, Wotton Underwood, Aylesbury.

Jimmy Smits ~~Milton Goldfarb Alan Rachins~~ Daniel Ziskie Aaron Seltzer Sandy McPeak ~~Jill Eikenberry~~ Jeremy Cox
~~Angela Picano~~ Max Templeton Julia Mortimer

~~...~~agne birthday
celebration in Chelsea.
Black and lacy frillies
are definitely out,
replaced by pastel-
coloured styles in silk.
But Reger fashion
doesn't come cheap. A
nightgown will set you
~~...~~

Sir Laurence Evans
ICM Ltd
388/396 Oxford Street
London W1N 9HE.

23rd June 1987.

Dear Sir Laurence,

Sue Green of your office - she sounds really sweet! - tells me that I completely misunderstood your letter of 17th June. I thought you were saying that Sir John Gielgud isn't worth us 100% on CRACK-UP, but Sue tells me that that isn't the case at all. Great! I think I must have been confused by the rather stuffed-shirt way in which you express yourself. Never mind - Sue and I get on brilliantly and I'm delighted to gather from her that Sir John is as keen as ever to play the part of the half-mad Duke of Dorset, subject, of course, to reading the script on his return from Israel.

I now enclose a copy of our standard PR form which Sue tells me I stupidly didn't enclose with my last letter! By the way - please tell Sir John not to bother to fill in the questions about 'involvement in previous scandals'. These are intended for the shady politicians and City celebrities who will be appearing as themselves or otherwise in the programme.

One last thing. You say that Rex Harrison isn't available to play the part of Prime Minister Macmillan in the series. Would he be available, by any chance, to play the part of the cabinet minister who is lowered from the ceiling on a kebab skewer? I'm having a terrible job casting this part. You don't happen to know who represents Robert Hardy, do you?

Yours sincerely,

Selina Sidey

Selina Sidey. Casting Dire[c]...

N M Rothschild & Sons Limited

PO Box No 185
New Court
St Swithin's Lane
London EC4P 4DU
(Registered Office)
Telephone 01-280 5000
Telex 888031
Direct Line

15th June 1987

our reference
your reference

Dear Ms. Picano,

This is to acknowledge your letter of 11th May and 25th May. Lord Rothschild tried to get into touch with Mr. Nicholas Coldstream but was unsuccessful. Can you by any chance let me know his home address?

At the present time Lord Rothschild does not feel able to deal with the matters you raised.

Yours sincerely,

Lorna Lindsay

Lorna Lindsay
Private Secretary

FILM AND TELEVISION COPYRIGHTS

139 Elm Park Mansions
Park Walk
London SW10

Tel: 01 − 352 9689
Telegrams: Concept London

Ms Lorna Lindsay
PO Box No 185
St Swithin's Lane
London, EC4P 4DU.

22nd June 1987.

Dear Ms Lindsay,

    Thank you for your letter of 15th June, which I am replying to on Miss Picano's behalf. Miss Picano has now left this company in circumstances which are in themselves 'suspicious'.

    First let me say what a relief it was to 'make contact' with Lord Rothschild, if only through a Box Number. We were becoming afraid that the Secretary of Pratts - Captain P.W.E. Parry MBE - was failing to forward mail to his members. We wrote to him on two occasions, accusing him of this, and received, I may say, a very impertinent response. (All is now sorted out, however, and we are shooting Miss Mandy Rice-Davies and a Mr Ivanov of the KGB at Pratts on the morning of Tuesday 11th July. If Lord Rothschild would like to 'sit in' on this, do please let me know.)

    Your failure to unearth a Mr Nicholas Coldstream at the Home Office is extremely disturbing. I'm afraid I don't know his home address. We wrote to the Home Office asking them for information on former security operatives for CRACK-UP and received his letter in return, a copy of which we sent to Lord Rothschild. Now we seem to have the case of 'the missing civil servant' on our hands! This, of course, will make an excellent scene in CRACK-UP.

    I look forward to hearing from you further.

Yours sincerely,

Daniel Ziskie. Producer.

cc.   Captain P.W.E. Parry MBE, Pratts.

Jimmy Smits ~~Milton Goldfarb~~ ~~Alan Rachins~~ Daniel Ziskie Aaron Seltzer Sandy McPeak ~~Jill Eikenberry~~ Jeremy Cox
~~Angela Picano~~ Max Templeton Julia Mortimer

FILM AND TELEVISION COPYRIGHTS

Miss Lizzie Wilkinson
The Publicity Director
The Stock Exchange
London, EC2N 1HP.

139 Elm Park Mansions
Park Walk
London SW10

Tel: 01 – 352 9689
Telegrams: Concept London

23rd June 1987.

Dear Lizzie,

Okay - let's you and me talk PR as per Sir Nicholas Goodison's letter of 1st June to our Mr Max Templeton (Development Editor) on CRACK-UP. We're delighted, needless to say, that Sir Nicholas has agreed to appear on the programme and I hope he was as chuffed as we were by the advance publicity I have so far obtained re his involvement (clippings enclosed). 'A Nation In The Dock', eh? Not bad!

I'd really like to breakfast you on this one, but I'm up to here in it at the moment. I'm enclosing instead one of our standard PR forms which I would like Sir Nicholas to fill in and return.

Our Executive Producer, Mr Aaron Seltzer, has asked me to say that when we interview Sir Nicholas on camera we would particularly like him to refute, if he can, the widespread notion that the City is now controlled by spivs in pin-stripes, that a gentleman's word isn't worth spit, that insider dealing and the spreading of false information to manipulate the markets are now rife and that drug-taking is so widespread among millionaires in short pants that the gent's toilet in many top City institutions is known as 'the Powder Room'.

We would like Sir Nicholas to muster his thinking in this area prior to transmission (we wouldn't want the red light to go on and him to be sitting there as if a stage weight's dropped on his head!) and we would also be grateful for any information he could give us on camera about the present standing in the City of the Midland Bank, the Chairman of Harrods and Sir Peter Carey of Morgan Grenfell. The latter, almost alone among City entrepreneurs, has behaved very oddly, consistently, and rudely, refusing to speak to us. Any information that Sir Nicholas can give us on film as to why this should be will be gratefully received (and entirely confidential).

I look forward to hearing from you, Liz.

Yours sincerely,

Sandy McPeak. Publicity Director.

THE STOCK EXCHANGE

Sandy McPeak
Publicity Director
Film and Television Copyrights
139 Elm Park Mansions
Park Walk
London SW10

Our ref: R/00/t

25 June 1987

Dear Mr McPeak

Thank you for your letter of 23rd of June, which has been passed
to me for reply. You appear to be under the mistaken impression
that Sir Nicholas Goodison had agreed to take part in the drama
documentary 'Crack Up'. Contrary to reports in the press (and
your own assumptions) at no time did Sir Nicholas or any of his
staff agree that he would be participating in the programme, or
suggest that we would 'talk PR' as you indicated in your letter.

I regret that we cannot be of any assistance.

Yours sincerely

Lizzie Wilkinson

Lizzie Wilkinson
Public Affairs Department

Registered Office:
The Stock Exchange, London EC2N 1HP
Telephone: 01-588 2355 Telex: 886557
Registered in England & Wales No.2075721

FILM AND TELEVISION COPYRIGHTS

139 Elm Park Mansions
Park Walk
London SW10

Tel: 01 – 352 9689
Telegrams: Concept London

The Rt Hon Cecil Parkinson MP
The House of Commons
London, SW1.

24th June 1987.

Dear Mr Parkinson,

I am disappointed that I haven't had an answer yet to my letter of 8th June with regard to you and Miss Jan Younger playing the parts of yourself and Miss Sara Keays in CRACK-UP.

In fact, since writing that letter we have had something of a change of mind, deciding now that you are perhaps a little too wooden in manner to portray yourself and that Miss Younger is not quite glamorous enough to make the love scenes acceptable to a sophisticated audience. After careful thought we have decided to replace the pair of you with Mr Gerald Harper and Miss Stefanie Marrian (photos enclosed).

I look forward to receiving your confirmation that both these excellent artistes meet with your approval.

With very best wishes.

Yours sincerely,

Selina Sidey

Selina Sidey. Casting Director.

STEFANIE MARRIAN

Cox

Jimmy Smits ~~Milton Goldfarb~~ ~~Alan Rachins~~ Daniel Ziskie Aaron Seltzer Sandy M...
Angela Picano Max Templeton Julia Mortimer

INTERNATIONAL CREATIVE MANAGEMENT, LTD.

DIRECTORS:
LAURENCE EVANS (CHAIRMAN)
DENNIS SELINGER (MANAGING)
MICHAEL ANDERSON

Jeremy Cox Esq.,
Film & Television Copyrights,
139 Elm Park Mansions,
Park Walk,
London SW10.   26th June, 1987.

Dear Mr. Cox,

                     "Crack-Up"

   Mr. Evans has asked me to say that, having re-read all the
correspondence and the synopsis, he understands the full impli-
cations of your project and of course he wishes you the very best
of luck.

   Mr. Evans feels that the short scenes you sent him cannot
possibly do justice to the full 10 hours of television.

   He also feels that work is needed to enrichen the rather
stark prose.

   A few years ago there was a certain Mr. Henry Root, a man of
considerable letters and extremely successful until, alas, he
tried to repeat his earlier success in a second book.

   Since that time we have lost track of him, but I do believe
that if he could be persuaded to do a polish on your screenplay
it would be to your advantage.

   If you feel there is anything to be gained by further
communication, Mr. Evans will be glad to hear from you.

        Yours sincerely,

        Sue Green
        Assistant to Laurence Evans

388/398, OXFORD STREET, LONDON, W1N 9HE.   TELEPHONE: 01-629 8080 · CABLE: INCREATIVE,LONDON · TELEX 885974
(REGISTERED OFFICE)   NEW YORK · LOS ANGELES · PARIS · ROME
                               EMPLOYMENT AGENCIES ACT 1973 LICENCE NO. SE (A) 2408   (REG. NO. 945898 ENGLAND)

                          A MEMBER OF THE Josephson TALENT AGENCY GROUP

CONSERVATIVE FAMILY CAMPAIGN

Bringing the family back into focus

45 West Hill Avenue, Epsom, Surrey KT19 8JX. Tel: 03727 21027.   Messages to: 01 677 9775

Chairman: Graham Webster-Gardiner   Hon. Secretary: Antonia Hopkins   Consultant: Dr. Adrian Rogers MB BS

24 June 1987

Mr Henry Root
139 Elm Park Mansions
Park Walk
LONDON SW10

Dear Sir

I am in receipt of your various recent communications. I
should have thought that it was obvious from the letter of
11 May, a copy of which I know you received, that you would
have appreciated that Conservative Family Campaign would not
be operating from that date until after the general election.
That therefore accounts for there being no replies to your
earlier correspondence. The delay in dealing with your most
recent letter of 11 June is for the same reason.

I am communicating with Peter Bruinvels to let him know of
your donation towards his campaign so that he may determine
what should be done with the money.

I have taken note of what you have said and enclosed.

Yours faithfully
CONSERVATIVE FAMILY CAMPAIGN

Graham Webster-Gardiner
Chairman

FILM AND TELEVISION COPYRIGHTS

139 Elm Park Mansions
Park Walk
London SW10

Tel: 01 – 352 9689
Telegrams: Concept London

Miss Mandy Perryment
The Penthouse Flat (all <u>right!</u>)
55 Onslow Gardens
London, SW7.

24th June 1987.

Dear Mandy,

    I was thrilled by your agent's news that you'd like to play the part of Mandy Rice-Davies in our super TV series CRACK-UP!

    I now enclose a couple of her best scenes, which I'm sure you'll love. MANDY has a couple of other good scenes, which I will get over to you just as soon as Nicholas Coleridge of Harpers & Queen has done some re-writes on them.

    I really look forward to meeting you.

    With best wishes.

    Yours,

Selina Sidey

    Selina Sidey. Casting Director.

...reak ~~Jill Eikenberry~~ Jeremy Cox
...ortimer

CRACK-UP. Episode 2. Scene 3. EXTERIOR. The swimming-pool at
Cliveden. Early evening. Present round the pool: CHRISTINE
KEELER, MANDY RICE-DAVIES, LORD ASTOR, PETER RACHMAN, STEPHEN
WARD, LORD BOOTHBY, THE KRAY TWINS, THE GREAT TRAIN ROBBERS,
BORIS IVANOV OF THE KGB, JOHN PROFUMO, MARY QUANT, etc.

WARD (to PROFUMO, pointing towards MANDY RICE-DAVIES): Not bad,
eh Jack?

PROFUMO: I should say so what! Quite a dolly bird! But a
touch - what? - obvious, don't you think? A bit common, do you
see? Damned if I don't prefer her.

WARD: Who?

PROFUMO: Her. Over there. Got more class what?

(PROFUMO points towards CHRISTINE KEELER).

WARD: Why don't you ask her for a swim, Jack?

PROFUMO: 'Pon my soul why not? (PROFUMO walks over to KEELER,
who is wearing a revealing swimsuit). Race you to the pool my
pretty little temptress!

KEELER: Ooooh! But you've still got all your clothes on,
Mr. Profumo!

PROFUMO: Not for long!

(PROFUMO takes off his ministerial three-piece and hands it to
STEPHEN WARD).

WARD (to KEELER): Take your swimsuit off. I think we've got a
turkey here.

KEELER: If you say so, darling. Here goes!

(KEELER undresses and poses by the poolside. She looks very
beautiful in the moonlight).

MANDY RICE-DAVIES: Silly tart.

BORIS OF THE KGB: My God! She's the loveliest thing I've ever
seen!

MANDY RICE-DAVIES: I'm not surprised. All the women in Moscow
look live Libby Purves.

TINA BROWN: I wish I'd said that.

MANDY RICE-DAVIES: You will, Tina, you will.

PROFUMO: I must have her! I must set her up in a Mayfair service
flat with a revolving water-bed and a Turkish masseuse!

ASTOR: Your career Jack! Have a care for God's sake!

PROFUMO: Fuck my career actually! I must have her! I'll buy
her a poodle and a wardrobe of customised clothes!

RICHARD WEST: He's ruled by his heart rather than his head.

CHRISTOPHER BOOKER: He'll pay his debt to society later.

PROFUMO: My boot-faced wife will stand by me in the blaze of unaccustomed publicity. I'll do community work in the East End. I'll attend even-song in country churches. Meanwhile I must have her!

(PROFUMO picks up the naked KEELER and runs with her towards the bushes).

WARD (calling out after him): Dig you later crocodile!

PROFUMO: In a while alligator!

(IVANOV OF THE KGB follows them into the bushes, camera clicking).

MAX HASTINGS: They're sitting on a political time-bomb.

LORD LAMBTON: In France, needless to say, a politician caught in his suspenders with two call-girls and a pimp on top of the wardrobe would go up in the electorate's estimation rather than down.

FADE.

CRACK-UP. Episode 2. Scene 8. INTERIOR. The Cabinet Room at
No 10 Downing Street. Late evening. Present: various MEMBERS
OF MACMILLAN's GOVERNMENT, AGENTS IN THE KGB, THE KRAY TWINS,
THE GREAT TRAIN ROBBERS, PETER RACHMAN, A RADDLED OLD DUCHESS,
THE BEATLES, STEPHEN WARD, CHRISTINE KEELER, MANDY RICE-DAVIES
and a selection of half-naked POULES DE NUITS cruising under the
surface of the Cabinet Meeting like hungry pike.

1st CABINET MINISTER (to KEELER): You're looking lovelier than
ever, my pretty little peach!

KEELER (simpering): Thank you, kind sir!

MANDY RICE DAVIES: Silly tart.

2nd CABINET MINISTER: Mandy! 'Pon my soul! It must be six
months!

MANDY RICE-DAVIES (looking him up and down scornfully): I thought
I told you to wait in the car.

2nd CABINET MINISTER: Ha! Ha! Don't you remember. It's me,
Reggie.

MANDY RICE-DAVIES (taking a closer look): So it is. I didn't
recognise you without your wallet.

STEPHEN WARD: For goodness sake control your wicked sense of
humour, Mandy. These are important people.

CHRISTOPHER BOOKER: He will be the victim of an historic injustice.

3rd CABINET MINISTER: Where's the Man In The Mask I say!

1st KGB AGENT: Here he comes now!

(4th CABINET MINISTER is lowered from the ceiling on a kebab skewer.
He is naked except for a mask, high heels and a suspender-belt.
All lash at him with napkins, Old Harrovian ties and Swaine Adeney
dressage whips. He howls with pleasure.)

4th CABINET MINISTER: Oh! Oh! Oh! Harder, I beg you, <u>harder</u>!

KEELER: You low, crawling, snivelling thing! Take that! And that!

RONNIE KRAY: And that!

4th CABINET MINISTER: Oh I say!

LORD BOOTHBY: I only met Ronnie Kray on one occasion, when he came
to my flat to discuss a charity function. I will not hesitate to
issue writs against anyone who alleges otherwise.

MANDY RICE-DAVIES: Otherwise.

LORD BOOTHBY: You will be hearing from Lord Goodman in the morning.

MANDY RICE-DAVIES: It's a good thing that I've got an
irrepressible sense of humour.

2nd KGB AGENT: Bring back capital punishment!

(Loud mutterings of 'Hear! Hear!' from the assembled red-necks.
The KRAY TWINS, THE GREAT TRAIN ROBBERS, etc, look alarmed.)

BUSTER EDWARDS: 'Ere! I don't like the sound of that!

CHARLIE WILSON: I think I'll 'ave it away on my toes!

RONNIE BIGGS: I'm off with a bosomy companion to Brazil.

(EDWARDS, WILSON and BIGGS exit).

PEREGRINE WORSTHORNE: They'll regret it. Better, by far, prison
on one's native soil than freedom abroad. The ancients were wiser
than us in recognising exile as the harshest punishment of all.
Perhaps Mr Ronnie Biggs, the celebrated train robber, will agree,
even as he basks on the sun-drenched beaches of Brazil with the
dusky maiden of his choice.

GEOFFREY WHEATCROFT: Apart from anything else, he'll find the
local wine quite intolerable. I have myself recently returned
from an agreeable mooch round the Dordogne area of France, not
least Conque, and.....

(THE CABINET MINISTERS have formed themselves into an unsteady
priapic pyramid.)

A.N. WILSON: Sex is the mysticism of materialists. This is the
decade when style gets the better of sense.

PRIME MINISTER MACMILLAN: I didn't know about any of this.

MANDY RICE-DAVIES: He would say that, wouldn't he?

FADE.

FILM AND TELEVISION COPYRIGHTS

139 Elm Park Mansions
Park Walk
London SW10

Tel: 01 – 352 9689
Telegrams: Concept London

24th June 1987.

Ms Jean Diamond
London Management
235 Regent Street
London W1A 2JT.

Dear Ms Diamond,

You will have heard of our super new TV series CRACK-UP, and I am now wondering whether your client Gerald Harper would like to appear in it as the Rt Hon Cecil Parkinson MP?

It's a smashing little part and there is already much press interest, of course, in who will play it.

If he's available, let me know and I'll send a couple of scenes over at once.

Yours sincerely,

Selina Sidey

Selina Sidey.

Dear Selina Sidey

Your letter about Crack up & Cecil Parkinson forwarded by Jean Diamond. In case I don't get to speak to her - yet it sounds very interesting - So what now?

Yours

Gerald Harper

GERALD HARPER
359 9108

Jimmy Smits Milton Goldfarb Alan h.   Angela

London Management
(LONDON MANAGEMENT & REPRESENTATION LTD.)
235/241 Regent Street London W1A 2JT   Telephone 01-493 1610   Telex 27498.
Cables Londent London W1   Fax (2 & 3): 01-408 0065

20th July, 1987

Ms Selina Sidey,
Film & Television Copyrights,
139 Elm Park Mansions,
Park Walk,
LONDON SW10

Dear Ms Sidey,

Further to your letter of 24th June regarding CRACK-UP and my client
GERALD HARPER, I am writing to say that Gerald is interested in principal
and I look forward to hearing from you further when you are ready to
discuss the matter fully.

Kind regards.

Yours sincerely,

Helen Filmer

JEAN DIAMOND

CHAIRMAN: Philip Parker FCA JOINT MANAGING DIRECTORS: William Marsh Dennis van Thal
...IVES: Marc Berlin LL.B. Nigel Britten Jean Diamond Richard Grenville Maureen Moore COMPANY SECRETARY: Roy Ros...
...ther Jeeves Kathleen Nathan Tony Peake VOICE OVER DEPT: Jackie Lane
...orated in England No. 624293   Member of the PMA   Licensed in accordance with the Employment Agencies Act 1973, Licence No. SE(A)1160

A.I.M.

Associated International Management Ltd
5 Denmark St., London WC2H 8LP
Tel: 01-836 2001

25th June 1987

Miss Selina Sidey
Film & TV Copyrights
139 Elm Park Mansions
Park Walk
London
SW10

Dear Selina,

Re: "CRACK UP"

Many thanks for your letter of the 19th June, Don Henderson would love to meet your director to discuss the project, although, I must say that with Don's schedule at the moment it might be a little difficult, however, if you could give me as much advance notice as you can, I will try and arrange things with the various production offices that Don is currently under contract to.

You mentioned in your previous letter that you thought the role of 'The Duchess Of Dorset' might not be good enough for VIRGINIA McKENNA, perhaps you would consider Don Henderson's wife SHIRLEY STELFOX who is currently to be seen starring opposite Julie Walters in the hit film **"PERSONAL SERVICES"** which is on general release at the moment.

I have asked both Jilly Johnson and Charlotte Seely if they are prepared to do scenes involving nudity and explicitness, and they have both agreed that they would. I have also asked another client **MISS SUE VANNER** and she also agreed, and so I am enclosing her details and pictures along with those of **SHIRLEY STELFOX**.

I look forward to hearing from you soon.

Yours sincerely

Derek

DEREK WEBSTER

Licensed in accordance with the employment agencies act 1973. Licensed No. SE8790. V.A.T. No. 417 6836 30.

VISION COPYRIGHTS

139 Elm Park Mansions
Park Walk
London SW10

Tel: 01 – 352 9689
Telegrams: Concept London

27th June 1987.

Mr Derek Webster
AIM
5 Denmark Street
London WC2H 8LP.

Dear Derek,

Many thanks for yours of 25th June with the really brilliant news that both Jilly Johnson and Charlotte Seely are keen to do scenes involving nudity and explicitness.

Just one thing: my assistant, Julia Mortimer, who was around in Jilly's hey-day in the late Sixties, says that she had – how can I put this? – rather neat bosoms. Jilly is my personal favourite to play the part of the nasty little tart Princess Soszynski, who, in the script, is always flaunting her tits, on which she had just had cosmetic surgery. Would Jilly, to get the part, consider a boob-job?

I very much look forward to hearing from you.

Yours,

Selina

Selina Sidey. Casting Director.

FILM AND TELEVISION COPYRIGHTS

139 Elm Park Mansions
Park Walk
London SW10

Tel: 01 – 352 9689
Telegrams: Concept London

The General Secretary
The Press Council
1 Salisbury Square
London EC4.

26th June 1987.

Dear Sir,

Hey – I've just been shit-bagged by two journalists on what I had hitherto assumed was quite a respectable paper – Mr Colin Randall of the Daily Telegraph and his boss (for the time being, I imagine) Mr Max Hastings.

Here's the story, sir: this company, as you will have heard, is currently developing a ten-part, £10 million TV series tracing the moral decline of this country from the Sixties to the present day.

Returning late to the office on the evening of 24th June I was door-stepped, if you please, by a man who has been sniffing round our premises for some time now and whom we have previously taken to be an MI5 operative (we're dealing with sensitive matters here). He looks, frankly, like the sort of man who might wear a bra to a lunch-time voucher party. A mouse, do you see? Bald but determined. Law and order, and MI5's reputation for disposal, being what they are these days, I ducked a confrontation with such a type and locked myself in the office john. For some time he stood outside, banging banging about and shouting threats, eventually shoving a piece of paper under the karzi door indicating that he was a journalist on The Daily Telegraph and had been sent round to mug us by his boss, Max Hastings. At first I was disinclined to believe him – nothing in The Telegraph's boastful advertising suggests that their stringers behave like Nigel Dempster – but after a while I thought I'd front the fellow up. To my amazement, he accused me of running a concert party here, of not seriously being in the business of developing a TV package! I don't have to tell you of the gravity of this charge or of the damage this company would suffer in terms of City credibility were such an accusation to appear in the press.

I would be grateful if you could let me know whether there have been many such complaints against the Telegraph since Hastings became Editor and also confirm that you are taking immediate action against him and his stringer Randall. I look forward to hearing from you.

Yours faithfully,

Daniel Ziskie. Producer.

cc. Mr Max Hastings.

Lord Mishcon, Lord Mishcon & Associates.

THE PRESS COUNCIL

No. 1 SALISBURY SQUARE, LONDON EC4Y 8AE

ESTABLISHED 1953
Tel: 01-353 1248

Chairman: RT HON SIR ZELMAN COWEN,
AK, GCMG, GCVO, QC
Director: KENNETH MORGAN, OBE

Please quote our reference: Y14717

Your reference:

FIRST CLASS
Mr Daniel Ziskie,
Film and Television Copyrights,
139 Elm Park Mansio ns,
Park Walk,
London SW10.

1 Jul 87.

Dear Mr Ziskie,

Thank you for your letter of 26 Jun 87 in connection with the conduct of the editor of the DAILY TELEGRAPH and reporter Mr Colin Randall.

I see that you have sent a copy of your letter to the editor and you may think it fair that he should have an opportunity to react to your complaint.

While the Press Council encourages editors to correspond directly with complainants, an intemperate letter such as the one you have sent is not the best way to open the correspondence.

If he does not contact you within a reasonable time - say seven days - or if you are dissatisfied with his response and believe the matter warrants investigation by the Council, you should write to the Director immediately to say so, enclosing copies of any further letters between you and the newspaper and any additional material you think may be helpful.

I enclose a leaflet explaining what the Council does and how to use its services in making a complaint.

In view of your action in sending a copy of your letter to a firm of solicitors, I should draw your attention to para 33, on the question of legal action.

Yours sincerely,

Neville Wareham,
Assistant Secretary.

Enc: Leaflet.

NUJ

NATIONAL UNION OF JOURNALISTS

ETHICS COUNCIL

Acorn House, 314-320 Gray's Inn Road, London WC1X 8DP Tel: 01-278 7916

Daniel Ziskie
Film & Television Copyrights
139 Elm Park Mansions
Park Walk
LONDON SW10

29 July 1987

Dear Daniel Ziskie,

Ethics Council complaint no.112

Your complaint was notified to the Ethics Council at its 29 July 1987
meeting.   The Ethics Council agreed that it should be investigated and I
will write to you again shortly when the panel processing the complaint
has met and let you know how they intend to proceed.

Please quote the above reference number in all future correspondence.

Yours sincerely,

Sally Gilbert

sj

FILM AND TELEVISION COPYRIGHTS

The Chairman
Harrods
Knightsbridge
London, SW1.

139 Elm Park Mansions
Park Walk
London SW10
Tel: 01 – 352 9689
Telegrams: Concept London

26th June 1987.

Dear Sir,

Disregard all info in previous letters concerning 'Major'
Randall of MI5. The fellow turns out to be nothing more sinister
than a stringer on The Daily Telegraph, stung, I suppose, at having
missed an exclusive re CRACK-UP! I should have identified him as
such, I suppose, from his shifty appearance.

I still look forward to hearing from you that our sensitive
material is safely deposited.

Yours faithfully,

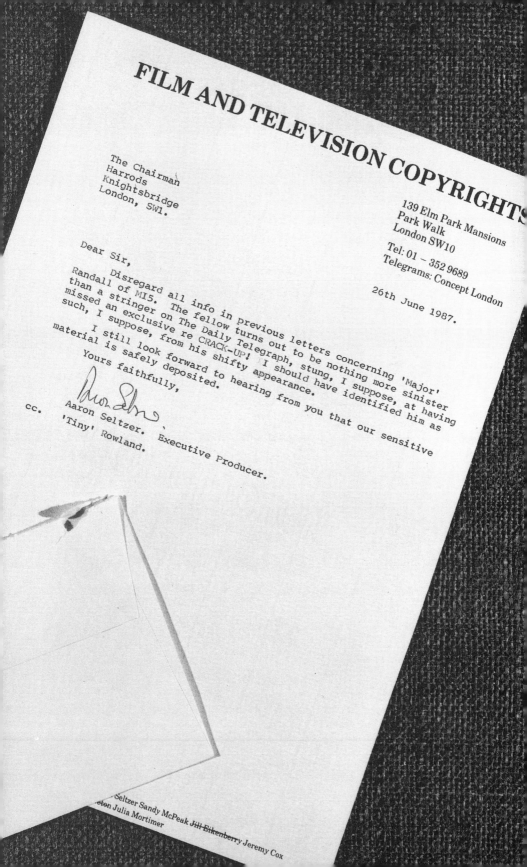

Aaron Seltzer. Executive Producer.

cc. 'Tiny' Rowland.

Seltzer Sandy McPeak Jill Eikenberry Jeremy Cox
ton Julia Mortimer

25 June 1987

Mr Daniel Ziskie
Film and Television Copyrights
139 Elm Park Mansions
Park Walk
London Sw10

Dear Mr Ziskie,

I have now had an opportunity to read your synopsis of CRACK-UP.
I must be frank, since you ask my opinion, and tell you that very
little of the dialogue has much ring of authenticity.

Could you please let me know whether the script is intended to
be humorous or serious. At the moment it sounds extremely parodic.

Yours sincerely,

Nicholas Coleridge
Editor

72 BROADWICK STREET LONDON W1V 2BP. 01-439 7144 A PUBLICATION OF THE NATIONAL MAGAZINE COMPANY LIMITED   REGISTERED OFFICE REGISTERED NUMBER 112955 ENGLAND
Telex: 263879 NATMAG G   Fax: 01-437 6886

FILM AND TELEVISION COPYRIGH

Nicholas Coleridge Esq
Harpers & Queen
72 Broadwick Street
London W1.

139 Elm Park Mansion
Park Walk
London SW10

Tel: 01 – 352 9689
Telegrams: Concept Londo

2nd July 1987.

Dear Coleridge,

Your letter of 25th June frankly amazed me. CRACK-UP is cert-ainly not parodic. It is barbed comedy. Not irreverent or whacky as such, merely barbed. Your ability to evaluate a script is clearly nil and I hereby rescind any offer made to you previously under a misapprehension as to your experience. Kindly return all material received from this office.

Yours sincerely,

Daniel Ziskie. Producer.

FILM AND TELEVISION COPYRIGHTS

139 Elm Park Mansions
Park Walk
London SW10

Tel: 01 – 352 9689
Telegrams: Concept London

Margaret, Duchess of Argyll
The Grosvenor House Hotel
Park Lane
London, W1.

29th June 1987.

Dear Duchess,

You will be glad to hear that Julia Mortimer's silly differences with this company have now been resolved – thanks to the intervention of a good friend (me!) – and that she is now back at work as my assistant.

Anyway, you will have gathered from all the really super press coverage that CRACK-UP has been getting that we are now hiring actors and actresses to play the parts of well-known people who for one reason or another – sometimes good, sometimes less good – want to keep a low profile for the moment. Since it is obviously important that these artistes bear a marked physical resemblance to the 'characters' they are impersonating we are seeking the approval of the latter before signing up the former. We certainly don't want to upset anyone unnecessarily!

Guess what! <u>No</u> big name wanted to play you! We offered the part to Mollie Sugden, Julie Walters, 'Boo' Laye, even to Jean Rook, but they all reacted angrily to the suggestion – rather as you did when we offered you the part of the drunken Duchess of Dorset! Luckily, a number of smaller agents made some quite sensible suggestions and we have now whittled the possibilities down to one – Miss Jean Campbell Dallas, whose photograph I am now enclosing with this letter for your approval.

Please let us know what you think as soon as possible, so that we can sign her up. We still hope to start shooting in September.

With very best wishes.
Yours sincerely,

Selina Sidey

Selina Sidey. Casting Director.

Enc. Photograph of Miss Jean Campbell Dallas.

JEAN CAMPBELL DALLAS

FILM AND TELEVISION COPYRIGHTS

139 Elm Park Mansions
Park Walk
London SW10

Tel: 01 – 352 9689
Telegrams: Concept London

Duncan Heath Esq
Duncan Heath Associates Ltd
Paramount House
162-170 Wardour Street
London W1V 3AT.

3rd July 1987

Dear Mr Heath,

Many thanks indeed for your letter of 26th June. We are all thrilled that Anthony Andrews is keen to play the part of the unpleasant, pop-eyed Marquis of Beauchamp in CRACK-UP and I now enclose some scenes for him to read.

I very much look forward to his reaction.

Yours sincerely,

Julia Mortimer

Julia Mortimer. Assistant to SELINA SIDEY.

DUNCAN HEATH ASSOCIATES LIMITED

Paramount House,
162-170 Wardour Street,
London W1V 3AT.

Telephone: 01-439 1471   Telex: 263361

26th June 1987

Julia Mortimer
Film and Television Copyrights
139 Elm Park Mansions
Park Walk
London
SW10

Dear Ms Mortimer

Thank you for your letter of 3rd regarding Anthony
Andrews and the forthcoming production of CRACK-UP.

Anthony is available during the period you mention
and would very much like to see the script. Perhaps
you would be good enough to send a copy to him c/o
this address.

Yours sincerely

Amanda Fowler

PP <u>Duncan Heath</u>

Registered Office,
Southwark Towers,
London Bridge Street,
London SE1 9SY.

Anthony Andrews   8th July 87.

Dear Julia Mortimer,
            Thank you so much for
allowing me to see a few scenes
from "Crack up".
            Sadly I don't think I can
play 28 any more!
            Thank you for the thought
it was an enjoyable read.
            Best regards

Anthony Andrews

FILM AND TELEVISION COPYRIGHT.

139 Elm Park Mansions
Park Walk
London SW10

Tel: 01 – 352 9689
Telegrams: Concept London

The Commissioner
The City of London Police
26 Old Jewry
London EC2.

3rd July 1987.

Dear Commissioner,

This is a courtesy letter to inform you that we will be filming certain scenes from our TV series CRACK-UP by HENRY ROOT in the environs of Throgmorton Street, Gracechurch Street and Fenchurch Street from 8am to 6pm on Monday 10th August.

Our set-up will consist of artistes (11), camera crew (34), production team (15 - including grip, chippy and continuity) plus mobile canteen and inter-office link-up system (GPO informed).

We are reluctant to interfere with traffic and normal police activity more than is absolutely necessary but we would be grateful if you could cordon off the above specified streets during the period of filming. We do not intend to hold up the normal flow of pedestrians since we intend to quiz commuters re drugs and City-slicker practices.

We would further be grateful if you would kindly arrange parking facilities in the area for our mobile canteen (54ft by 20ft). By trade union custom, crew, artistes, chippies, grips etc are entitled to refreshment between takes on a more regular basis than old-fashioned Tories like you and I, Commissioner, might deem strictly professional.

You will recall that in my letter to you of 26th May I invited you to participate yourself in CRACK-UP and now wonder whether you have yet reached a decision on this. Many leading City figures have already agreed to cooperate, as the attached clippings from 'Today' and 'The Sunday Times' will show, I think. I am not suggesting that those who have turned us down - like Sir Peter Carey of the beleaguered merchant bank Morgan Grenfell plc - necessarily have something to hide, but it doesn't look good, I think you'll agree.

I very much look forward to hearing from you with the necessary permissions and with your agreement to appear on film yourself.

Yours sincerely,

Daniel Ziskie. Producer.

TELEPHONE: 01- 601 2222

EXT.

TELEGRAMS: ADJUTOR. LONDON. TELEX

OFFICIAL LETTERS TO BE ADDRESSED:-
THE COMMISSIONER OF POLICE
FOR THE CITY OF LONDON

PLEASE QUOTE REF.

YOUR REF.

CITY OF LONDON POLICE

"A" Department
37 Wood Street
London EC2V 7HN

A/F4/199/87

10 July 1987

Mr D Ziskie
Executive Producer
Film & Televison Copyrights
139 Elm Park Mansions
Park Walk
London SW10

Dear Sir

I have received your letter of 3rd July, 1987, regarding your proposed filming activities in the vicinity of Throgmorton Street on 10th August, 1987.

I am very sorry to have to inform you that it will not be possible to relax the guidelines referred to in Form 60. With about 400 applications to film in the street being made to this Force every year it would place us in a most difficult position if exceptions were made for your company.

In particular, the police may only close streets to traffic if the law permits. I regret that there is no power for the police to close streets for filming and any attempt to do so would be illegal.

As far as parking is concerned, it may be possible to permit a limited amount of parking in the area with the exception of canteen and refreshment vehicles. Experience shows that the obstruction and inconvenience caused by this type of vehicle during the normal business hours of the City makes their presence unacceptable.

I would refer you to paragraph 4(d) of Form 60 and ask you to consider changing the day of your filming to a weekend when it might be possible to offer more assistance with your parking problem.

I would like you to arrange a site meeting between one of your staff and Mr.John Daughters of my Functions Office when the parking arrangements can be discussed in more detail.

Yours faithfully,

John Cardwell

Chief Superintendent

The Duke of Roxburghe
Floors Castle
Kelso
Scotland.

Park Walk
...Mansions
London SW10

Tel: 01 – 352 9689
Telegrams: Concept London

5th July 1987.

Your Grace,

Many thanks for your letter of 29th June. I must admit I'm rather intrigued by your suggestion that you should, as you say, tell us 'the true story' of the courtship between the Duke and Duchess of York at your historic home. I was a little surprised that you should think it proper that you should so so, but if you're happy, then so are we!

Strangely enough we had indeed intended to include Andy and Fergie's courtship in our series (to illustrate the informality with which the younger Royals now conduct their affairs) and to this end have paid a lot of money for the worldwide rights in 101 THINGS YOU DIDN'T KNOW ABOUT THE ROYAL LOVEBIRDS by Talbot Church (Pan Books, £2.50). Have you read it? It's absolutely super. Anyway – I now enclose a photostat passage from the book and wonder, in the first place, whether you could check this for accuracy? We wouldn't want to dramatise this without being satisfied that it is correct in every detail. Is it true, for instance, that your family motto is: 'Softly Softly Catchee Monkey'?

You don't mention money in your letter. Perhaps you could let me know what fee (not too steep, I hope!) you would think appropriate were you to act as technical adviser on all scenes involving members of the Royal Family.

I'm _really_ looking forward to working with you on this!

Yours sincerely,

Selina Sidey. Developm...

---

101 Things You Didn't Know

Birds remember in detail the moment
Andrew went down on both knees in the
of Floors Castle, took his love's hand in
the question. Sarah, her mane of red hair
shoulders, blushed and said, 'Yes!'
astle in the Scottish borders, set in 60,000
anks of the River Tweed and used by
rs for the Tarzan film *Greystoke*, has long
ary for love-lorn royals.
halls, draped with the flags and armour of a
Prince Charles wooed his bride, Lady
ter Andrew dallied with blue-movie actress

weekend of February, as the rain poured
de and their hosts, the Duke and Duchess of
e (family motto – 'Softly Softly Catchee
kept discreetly out of the way, the Sailor
the Major's daughter decided to marry.
ad travelled to her assignation in great secret.
f at the castle had not been told the identity of
g couple who came to stay. It was only as Sarah
back to London that she was spotted leaving
tle Airport using the name 'Miss Oxford' – an
omment by the irrepressible Major's daughter on
that blue-movie actress Koo Stark used to call
'Miss Cambridge' when flying to Mustique with
oyal Romeo!

Don't forget the fruitgums, Fergie! Now a member of the Royal Family, Major Ronnie Ferguson still does his shopping at the village store. 'There's nothing stuffy about Major Ronnie,' says genial shopkeeper, 83-year-old Edith Parker.

From: The Duke of Roxburghe

FACTOR
P. F. L. Batchelor, B.Sc. F.R.I.C.S.
Telephone Kelso (0573) 23333

Roxburghe Estates Office
Kelso
Roxburghshire
TD5 7SF

Miss Selina Sidey,
Development Editor,
Film and Television Copyrights,
139 Elm Park Mansions,
Park Walk,
London SW10

20th July 1987

Dear Miss Sidey,

I write in response to your letter dated July 5th.

I have no record or memory of writing any letter to you along the lines to which you refer in your letter, so therefore must assume that there is some mistake or that someone has written to you under false pretences.

Your initial feeling that I would not be involved in any confirmation of reported events is indeed accurate, and I confirm that I cannot be of any assistance in correcting any script you may produce.

I would appreciate an answer in writing that you have received this letter.

Yours sincerely,

Roxburghe

---

101 Things You Didn't Know

56

Before her present job, career-girl Fergie was an editor at songsmith Tim Rice's publishing house, Pavilion Books. 'All we did in those days were picture books and celebratory volumes of dead film stars by Alexander Walker. Fergie changed all that – the first book she commissioned, in the face of determined opposition in-house, was *Neil's Book of the Dead*. We all thought she was crazy at the time but then *The Young Ones* took off and it turned out to be the biggest seller in Pavilion's history.'

But on-the-move Fergie stayed a mere nine months at Pavilion. 'She was ambitious and there was a certain amount of jealousy here, particularly with her being a woman', commented her former colleague. 'We certainly miss her.'

About the Royal Love Birds

In November 1984, an unusual inci
on the Prince's extraordinary
indifference to pain. One evening
he wandered into Prince Charl
found the future king condu
matter' experiments with a g
Indians – levitating, sitting on
through their noses and so fo

Try-anything-once Andre
discovered that he could si
longer than the fakirs cou
physiologist was consulted
Condition. In sufferers fro
from different parts of th
slowly than they do in no
his finger, for instance, b
long as five minutes, by
incident and he will carr

In a fit young man, th
itself in feats of extraor
broken bones should
serious, and it was t
Prince would have
escapades.

Fortunately, a le
many was brought
rigorous tests, it w
from Smith's C
exceptionally bra

FILM AND TELEVISION COPYR[IGHT]

139 Elm Park Mansions
Park Walk
London SW10

Tel: 01 – 352 9689
Telegrams: Concept London

23rd July 1987.

The Duke of Roxburghe
Roxburghe Estates Office
Kelso
Roxburghshire.

Dear Duke,

Your letter of 20th July to our Selina Sidey has been passed over to me for action (I'm in charge of PR here). 'I have no memory of writing to you along the lines to which you refer', you say, which makes me suppose that you wrote to us along different lines and that there was a typing mistake by your secretary. It would be a great help if you could now send us a copy of the letter you meant to send in the first place.

I now enclose another passage from 101 THINGS YOU DIDN'T KNOW ABOUT THE ROYAL LOVEBIRDS by Talbot Church - The Man Who Knows The Royals - and would be most grateful if you could, as a friend of the young couple, confirm or deny the rumour that the Duke suffers from Smith's Condition. I certainly don't want to trouble the Lovebirds with this one.

I would further be grateful for your views on a story in last week's Sunday Times Colour Supplement by Royal Writer Georgina Howell. Ms Howell says that during a game of Royal Blind Man's Buff during their courtship at your historic home, Prince Andrew, as he then was, hid under a table and the Duchess of York, as she then wasn't, proceeded to identify him by the seat of his pants!

Ms Howell wrote: '"Steady on!" joked Andy irrepressibly, "you can't touch the Royal bum yet!" Everyone collapsed with laughter, of course, and the Royal Romance was on!'

Could you confirm that this hilarious snatch of dialogue did actually occur?

I look forward to hearing from you.

Yours sincerely

Sandy McPeak. Publicity Director.

PS. We would, of course, like to film the scenes featuring Andy an[d] Fergie at your castle. Could you let me know when it would be convenient for Selina and I to pop up there for a weekend do do some preliminary research?

57

w some light
d complete
gham Palace,
rs, where he
e 'mind over
orange-sheeted
putting needles

and it was soon
ted gas-ring for
ley Street neuro-
diagnosed Smith's
Condition, signals
ach the brain more
e. If a sufferer pricks
t feel anything for as
e he has forgotten the
othing has happened.
n is trivial, manifesting
rage. In later life, when
immediately, it is more
first that the dare-devil
t his more hair-raising

rophysiologist from Ger-
r further, and much more
red that Andew didn't suffer
all, but was simply quite

my Smits Milton Goldfarb Alan Rachins Daniel Ziskie Aaron Seltzer Sandy McPeak Jill Eikenberry Jeremy Co[
Angela Picano Max Templeton Julia Mortimer

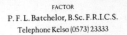

FACTOR
P. F. L. Batchelor, B.Sc. F.R.I.C.S.
Telephone Kelso (0573) 23333

From: The Duke of Roxburghe

Roxburghe Estates Office
Kelso
Roxburghshire
TD5 7SF

Sandy McPeak, Esq.,
PR Director,
Film and Television Copyrights,
139 Elm Park Mansions,
Park Walk,
London SW10.

31st July 1987

Dear Mr. McPeak,

I am replying to your letter of July 23rd.

As I indicated in my letter of July 20th I have no recollection of writing to Ms. Selina Sidey at any stage. I repeat that I will not be involved with confirming or denying anything connected to the Royal Family and I will not agree to any scenes being filmed at Floors Castle or the grounds.

I trust that there will be no further communication on this matter.

Yours faithfully,

Roxburghe

FILM AND TELEVISION COPYRIGHT

The Duke of Roxburghe
Roxburghe Estates Office
Kelso
Roxburghshire.

139 Elm Park Mansions
Park Walk
London SW10

Tel: 01 – 352 9689
Telegrams: Concept London

2nd August 1987.

Dear Duke,

Many thanks indeed for your letter of 31st July. I note that you will deny nothing concerning the Royal Love Birds, so I'm taking this as a 'yes' on Smith's Condition and the game of Royal Blind Man's Buff.

Please let me know as soon as possible when it would be convenient for Selina and I to pop up for the weekend.

With best wishes.

Yours sincerely,

Sandy McPeak. Publicity Director.

FILM AND TELEVISION COPYRIGHTS

Mr Cobden Ramsey
Radcliffe's
10 Little College Street
London, SW1.

139 Elm Park Mansions
Park Walk
London SW10

Tel: 01 – 352 9689
Telegrams: Concept London

4th July 1987.

Dear Cobden,

It was a relief, I must say, to get your phone call yesterday in the matter of Margaret, Duchess of Argyll. As I explained, our Casting Director (Miss Selina Sidey) is in meetings in the United States until next Thursday, 9th July, so I am dealing with the matter until her return.

Now that the Duchess has put her affairs into the hands of professionals, perhaps we will be able to talk turkey at last. Quite frankly, dealing with the Duchess has been something of a headache. We're mounting a £10 million TV series here, Cobden, but she's been treating the matter like a society tea-party (no offence meant).

What we want is very simple – merely that she should now give us the go-ahead to sign that fine actress Miss Jean Campbell Dallas to play her in the series (as per our letter of 29th June) and that she should fill in and return to our Mr Sandy McPeak (Publicity) the PR form – previous experience, real name, hobbies, amusing anecdotes etc – enclosed in the same letter.

I look forward to hearing from you as soon as possible. We aim to shoot the Duchess in late September and because of her unprofessional attitude to date we are now dangerously behind schedule.

Perhaps I could take this opportunity to ask you whether you have other artistes on your books who might be suitable for some of the smaller parts (all the leads have now been cast). To assist you in this I now enclose a synopsis of the series and a cast breakdown. All your suggestions would be most welcome, but Julia Mortimer (Assistant Casting Director) has asked me to say that we are having a lot of trouble finding someone to play the Cabinet Minister on the kebab skewer. Do you by any chance happen to represent Frank Bough?

Yours sincerely,

Daniel Ziskie.

Enc. CRACK-UP. Synopsis and cast breakdown.

PRUDENTIAL

Ms Julia Mortimer
Executive Producer
Film and Television Copyrights
139 Elm Park Mansions
Park Walk
SW10

The Prudential Assurance
Company Limited
142 Holborn Bars
London EC1N 2NH

F B Corby
Chairman
Direct line 01-936 0202

18 June 1987

Dear Ms Mortimer

I acknowledge your letter of 7 June regarding the Prudential's current TV
commercial featuring Griff Rhys-Jones.

I must say I and my colleagues are surprised at your reaction to what we
consider to be a most inoffensive advertisement: we have had no other
reactions remotely similar to your own.

You have extended an invitation to appear in a programme "tracing the moral
decline of this country". Having regard particularly to the way your letter
is expressed, we do not wish to take part.

Yours sincerely

Part of Prudential Corporation
Incorporated and Registered in England Registered office as above Registered number 15454

FILM AND TELEVISION COPYRIGHTS

139 Elm Park Mansions
Park Walk
London SW10

Tel: 01 – 352 9689
Telegrams: Concept London

Mr F.B. Corby
The Prudential Assurance Company Ltd
142 Holborn Bars
London EC1 2NH.

6th July 1987.

Dear Corby,

<u>CRACK-UP</u>.

I am taking it upon myself to reply to your rude letter of
18th June. We are all extremely surprised that you responded in
the way you did to Miss Mortimer's closely reasoned argument.
Everyone we have spoken to agrees with her that your commercial
featuring the little TV comedian is exceptionally offensive.

The writer of our series, in fact, has now inserted a very
amusing new scene in which you and your advertising associates are
planning an audaciously sexist campaign, auditioning 'models' to
participate with 'perks' offered (visits to the Costa Brava etc with
disgusting old men, as per the objectionable commercials).

We think that it would greatly benefit our series were you to
play the part of yourself in this scene. If you would like to read
a copy of the script before making up your mind, please let me know.
It is a short scene, but it makes its point skilfully, I think. If
you are unwilling to appear as yourself, we will engage an actor to
play you - first gaining your approval, of course, as to his suit-
ability.

I look forward to hearing from you - with a positive response,
I hope.

Yours sincerely,

Daniel Ziskie.

PRUDENTIAL
CORPORATION

D M Vevers
Public Affairs Manager
Direct line 01-936 8722

Mr D Ziskie
Executive Producer
Film and Television Copyrights
139 Elm Park Mansions
Park Walk
London SW10

9 July 1987

Dear Mr Ziskie

We acknowledge receipt of your letter of 6 July addressed to Mr Corby.
As Mr Corby is away on holiday at the moment I am responding to your
letter.

We have tried on numerous occasions to make contact with you by
telephone, but the number quoted on your letter heading seems to be
permanently connected to an answering machine and we have been unable
to talk to anyone.

We do not agree that the television commercial to which you refer is
offensive in any way whatsoever. It is a humorous advertisement
featuring a well known television comedian. We have had no complaints
about it being sexist from any other source. This particular
commercial has now been seen by some 20 million people and you are the
only person to have raised this extraordinary suggestion. Where you
find reference to "perks offered (visits to the South of France etc)"
we have no idea, there are no such references to that in the commercial
either implicit or explicit.

I can advise you that Mr Corby will certainly not be prepared to appear
in the scene in your film and, in fact, should you continue to propose
such a scene, which is highly offensive to Mr Corby and totally
inaccurate as to the Prudential's aims and objectives, then we must
consult our lawyers in order to take the appropriate action.

Yours sincerely

David M Vevers
D0708E

Prudential Corporation plc
142 Holborn Bars London EC1N 2NH Tel 01-405 9222 Telex 8811419 Fax 01-936 0038
Incorporated and Registered in England Registered office as above Registered number 1397169

FILM AND TELEVISION COPYRIGHTS

139 Elm Park Mansions
Park Walk
London SW10

Mr David Vevers
Prudential Corporation plc
142 Holborn Bars
London EC1 2NH.

Tel: 01 – 352 9689
Telegrams: Concept London

10th July 1987.

Dear Mr Vevers,

Thank you for your letter of 9th July with regard to your offensive commercial featuring Mr Griff Rhys-Jones the TV comedian.

You say that you have made frequent attempts to reach us on the telephone but could only get the answering-machine. We are making a £10 million TV series here, David, not sitting around the office drinking cups of tea and auditioning topless lovelies for sexist TV commercials. We're out there shooting. The point of an answering-machine is that you should leave a message on it. Had you done so, we might have rung you back.

I am surprised that you should resort to a show-of-hands argument re the offensiveness or otherwise of your TV commercial. 'The News Of The World' is read by twenty million people but you would not on that account, I take it, want to argue that it's not offensive. Let me know.

I am sorry that Corby will not wish to appear as himself in our series – though how you can know this when he is away on holiday I'm not quite sure. I will take your word for it temporarily, however, and now have pleasure in enclosing a photograph of the actor whom we would like to engage for the part – Mr Jeff Pirie – but we will not sign him up, of course, until we have received Corby's go-ahead.

I am surprised by the threat of 'appropriate action' by your lawyers. So? You expect us to take that lying down? We ourselves have smart lawyers working round the clock. Such a threat before you have even read the script appears somewhat neurotic, if I may say so, and suggests to me that you yourself have grave doubts as to the good taste or otherwise of your current advertising.

I look forward to hearing from you.

Yours sincerely,

Daniel Ziskie. Producer.

Mr D Ziskie
Executive Producer
Film and Television Copyrights
139 Elm Park Mansions
Park Walk
London SW10

D M Vevers
Public Affairs Manager
Direct line 01-936 8722

Dear Mr Ziskie

Thank you for your letters of 10 and 25 July.

I can confirm that Mr Corby himself is not prepared to appear in the proposed scene in your film, nor does he give his "go-ahead" for you to engage Mr Pirie for the part, or indeed any other actor whom you might wish to propose.

In view of the tone of your earlier letters, it appears that your proposed scene would be both offensive and totally inaccurate as to the Prudential's aims and objectives. If you were to go ahead with it and if this were to turn out to be the case, then certainly we would consult our lawyers in order to take the appropriate action.

Yours sincerely

David M Vevers

TELEPHONE: 01 583 0777
TELEX: 862687 (BRICK G)
FAX: 01-583 9401 (Group 3)

1, BRICK COURT,
TEMPLE,
LONDON EC4Y 9BY

Daniel Ziskie, Esq.
Film and Television Copyrights
139 Elm Park Mansions
Park Walk
London SW10

8th July 1987

Dear Mr. Ziskie,

Thank you for your letter of 7th July.

I assume you will have seen a letter I wrote to The Times on Friday, 3rd July, which explains fully why I defended Geoffrey Collier. I do not think there are "allegations inevitably falling about" my head, and I dislike the suggestion that anyone who declines to be interviewed could create the suspicion that there is something to hide.

Having set out the full position, I do not see any need to repeat my explanation by appearing in your programme.

Yours sincerely,

for   Robert Alexander QC

FILM AND TELEVISION COPYRIGHTS

139 Elm Park Mansions
Park Walk
London SW10

Tel: 01 – 352 9689
Telegrams: Concept London

Hugh P. Stewart
Westland plc
Yeovil
Somerset BA20 2YB.

10th July 1987.

Dear Stewart,

    I am amazed at the reception we received yesterday when attempting to get our camera crew and production facilities past your main gate in order to film Sir John Cuckney.

    You were well aware of the cost to us of transporting same all the way to Weston-super-Mare, and we must now, of course, charge this amount to you.

    I have sent an itemised statement to your Accounts Department (copy enclosed) and must inform you that unless this sum is remitted within one week we will be compelled to hand the matter over to our solicitor for collection.

    That said, and over-looking Sir John's neurotic attitude to explaining himself on film, we still intend to feature him in our series - CRACK-UP: A NATION IN THE DOCK! - and I now enclose a photograph of Mr Lee Crawford, the actor we wish to cast as Sir John. I would be grateful if you could let me know whether he meets with Sir John's approval.

    Yours sincerely,

Daniel Ziskie.   Executive Producer.

Enc.   Photograph of Mr Lee Crawford.

NEVILLE TAYLOR

Jimmy Smits Milton Goldfarb Alan Rachins Daniel Ziskie
Angela Picano Max Ter

FILM AND TELEVISION COP...

139 Elm Park Mansions
Park Walk
London SW10

Tel: 01 – 352 9689
Telegrams: Concept London

10th July 1987.

The Accounts Department
Westland plc
Yeovil
Somerset.

INVOICE.

To cost of transporting full production facilities to Yeovil to
film Sir John Cuckney on 9th July 1987 as per agreement dated 1st
June 1987 (copy enclosed) - diesel, crew (31), cameramen, make-up,
sound, grip, chippy, accountant, production staff, producer, directo
assistant director, carpenter, mobile canteen, stylists, 2nd unit
director, catering staff, Equity observer..................£7,865.44

Kindly Remit.

FILM AND TELEVISION COPYRIGHTS

139 Elm Park Mansions
Park Walk
London SW10

Tel: 01 – 352 9689
Telegrams: Concept London

11th July 1987.

Hugh P. Stewart
Westland plc
Yeovil
Somerset BA20 2YB.

Dear Hugh,

Oh dear! I'm afraid that our Mr Ziskie, when writing to you
yesterday enclosed the wrong photograph of the actor playing Sir
John in our series! Not really his fault. Casting isn't his department and he should have left it to me. Anyway - he sent a pho
of Mr Nevile Taylor, the really super actor who is playing Zaphyr
the cheery coke dealer in CRACK-UP, instead of a photo of Mr Lee
Crawford, who is, of course, playing Sir John. I now enclose Mr
Crawford's photo and hope he meets with Sir John's approval.

With very best wishes.

Yours,

Selina Sidey. Casting Director.

Westland Group plc

YEOVIL ENGLAND BA20 2YB

TELEPHONE: YEOVIL 0935 75222
FAX: 0935 702131/702133
TELEX: 46277 WHL YEO G

DIRECT LINE: 702018

Our Ref: S/JRB/PG/6466

Your Ref:

Date: July 24, 1987

Mr. D. Ziskie,
Film and Television Copyrights,
139, Elm Park Mansions,
Park Walk,
LONDON SW10

Dear Sir,

　　Your letter and invoice dated 10th July 1987 have been passed to me.

　　In my view there is no legal basis whatsoever for your claim. If legal proceedings are brought they will be vigorously contested.

Yours faithfully,

(J.R. Bayley)
Group General Counsel

Registered Office Yeovil, England, BA20 2YB Registered number 302632 England

FILM AND TELEVISION COPYRIGHTS

139 Elm Park Mansions
Park Walk
London SW10

Tel: 01 – 352 9689
Telegrams: Concept London

Mr J.R. Bayley
Westland Group plc
Yeovil
Somerset.

27th July 1987.

Dear Bayley,

    I am thunder-struck by your letter of 24th July and attitude
to an invoice properly rendered.

    We have no doubt that our request for reimbursement of monies
correctly spent through your company's haphazard regard for shooting
schedules is water-tight in a court of law.

    Since it is your clear tactic to stonewall on this one, hoping,
no doubt that we will wither on the vine, I must tell you that we
don't roll over that easily.

    In the circumstances I must ask you now to inform me of the
name of your attorneys so that we may serve proceedings.

    Alternatively, we might be prepared to <u>share</u> with you the
accumulated costs to date (plus interest) were Sir John prepared
to make a new date for filming. Needless to say, we would not wish
to transport artistes and facilities all the way to Somerset only
to be buggered around a second time. Please let me know whether you
think this might be a commercial solution to our suit against you.

    Yours sincerely,

Danile Ziskie. Producer.

Westland Group plc

YEOVIL ENGLAND BA20 2YB

Our Ref: S/JRB/PG/6472

Your Ref:

Date: July 28, 1987

Mr. D. Ziskie,
Film and Television Copyrights,
139, Elm Park Mansions,
Park Walk,
LONDON SW10

Dear Sir,

I refer to your letter of 27th July. Our solicitors, who are authorised to accept service of proceedings, are Slaughter & May (Attention Mr. J. Hine) 35 Basinghall Street, London EC2V 5DB.

I would advise you that Sir John Cuckney is not, and never has been, prepared to make any date with you for filming or to be involved in any way whatsoever in your project.

Yours faithfully,

(J.R. Bayley)
Group General Counsel

FILM AND TELEVISION COPYRIGHTS

139 Elm Park Mansions
Park Walk
London SW10

Tel: 01 – 352 9689
Telegrams: Concept London

Mr J.R. Bayley
Westland Group plc
Yeovil
Somerset.

31st July 1987.

Dear Bayley,

So! I'm impressed! Slaughter & May, eh? And when did they ever persuade a jury to find for Jeffrey Archer? I suppose you think we'll be represented by some bubble-head in her first year at law school. No sir - our solicitor is none other than Lord Mishcon. How do you like them apples?

You will be hearing from him shortly, I have no doubt.

Yours sincerely,

Daniel Ziskie.

cc.   Lord Mishcon, Victor Mishcon & Co.

FILM AND TELEVISION COPYRIGHTS

139 Elm Park Mansions
Park Walk
London SW10

Tel: 01 – 352 9689
Telegrams: Concept London

The Secretary
The Reform Club
104 Pall Mall
London, SW1.

15th July 1987.

Dear Sir or Madam,

You will recall that a Miss Paula Yates (now Lady Geldof) posed starkers at your club in 1979, the photos appearing later in Knave magazine. I thought they were pretty gross, but I suppose all the publicity was good for you, drumming up lots of new members and so forth. Anyway - we've decided to re-enact the incident in a ten-part TV series called CRACK-UP as an example of this country's sad decline into sleaze and corruption under Mrs Thatcher.

I know what you're thinking: you're thinking 'Good God! Surely Lady Geldof's far too old these days to bounce around in public without her clothes!' - and you're right, of course, as Lady Geldof herself is the first to admit. She will merely be acting as technical adviser on the scene and we have employed a really super young model called Jilly Johnson (photo enclosed) to play her.

We would like to shoot the scene in late August or early September, so I would be grateful if you could let me know which date would suit you best. We will inconvenience you as little as possible, using only a skeleton crew of some two dozen - sound, grip, stylists, Equity observer etc (Plouviez has indicated that he'd like to be on this one personally). If some of your members would like to appear on film as unpaid extras - sitting around, snoozing, boozing, boggling etc - as they did when Lady Geldof was originally shot, we would have no objections. Indeed it would help us were the activities of the club to proceed as normally as possible.

I look forward to hearing from you.

Yours sincerely,

Selina Sidey

Selina Sidey. Locations Manager.

TELEPHONE:
01-930 9374.
(7 LINES)

PLEASE ADDRESS ALL
COMMUNICATIONS TO
THE SECRETARY

REFORM CLUB,

PALL MALL,

SWIY 5EW

17th. July, 1987.

Miss S. Sidey, .
Location Manager,
FILM AND TELEVISION COPYRIGHTS,
139, Elm Park Mansions,
Park Walk,
LONDON.   S.W.10.

Dear Madam,

    I write to acknowledge your unsigned letter dated 15th.July,
1987, in which you seek permission to film some sequences in the
Club.

    I have to advise you that your request is declined and I am
returning, as you asked, the press cuttings you enclosed with
your letter.

               Yours faithfully,

                  SECRETARY.
                  R.A.M.FORREST.

CRACK-UP by HENRY ROOT.

Inter-Office Memo.

Date: 16th July 1987.

Time: 4.45pm.

From: Jimmy Smits to Aaron Seltzer.

For fuck's sake, Aaron, what's going on? I've just received a
phone call from a Woman Detective Sergeant Wilson at Bow Street
Police Station saying that she wants to interview you urgently
about a forged letter she says you sent to the Duchess of Argyll.
What the hell was that?

CRACK-UP by HENRY ROOT.

Inter-Office Memo.

Date: 17th July 1987.

Time: 10.15am.

From: Aaron Seltzer to Jimmy Smits.

I'll tell you what the hell it was, Jimmy. It was the letter you
told me to forge on solicitor's writing-paper when we were trying
to stop the Duchess of Argyll suing us over the Mortimer business.
The old trout must have gone to the cops. (Forged letter enclosed).

CRACK-UP by HENRY ROOT.

Inter-Office Memo.

Date: 17th July 1987.

Time: 11.50 am.

From: Jimmy Smits to Aaron Seltzer.

Christ Almighty, Aaron, forgery's a serious offence. The last thing
we want at the moment is for you to be hauled downtown in bracelets.
We're dead meat here if Lindsey Anderson gets to hear of this.
I suggest you 'disappear' for a while. I'll get the Mortimer woman
to stall Woman Detective Sergeant Wilson for as long as possible.
If this gets serious, we can pack up and go, leaving Mortimer holding the stick by the dirty end.

ESSEX HOUSE
ESSEX STREET
STRAND
LONDON WC2R 3AQ

DAY   01-836 8333
NIGHT 01-836 5566
HICKSOLOR LONDON WC2
TELEX 22533

4 RUE D'ANJOU
PARIS VIII

265 1304
TELEX 66853

JOHN L. KIRKCONEL
JOHN E. PAYNE
GORDON D. CALDWELL
HAROLD HORSFALL-TURNER, C.B.E.
GEOFFREY L. WICKS
ANTHONY J. H. WICKENS
PAUL R. DAVIES
TIMOTHY J. L. COX
JULIE A. SCOTT-BAYFIELD
NICHOLAS N. J. SMITH
DAVID A. CRICK
PHILIP J. A. HAWKES
ROY A. FURNESS
DOROTHY E. F. CLIFFORD
JAMES BURNETT-HITCHCOCK
MICHAEL HUDSON
M. CHARLOTTE CROOK
GRAHAM N. RUMNEY
PETER S. BISHOP

9th June 1987.

42/OAR

Mr Aaron Seltzer
Film and Television Copyrights
139 Elm Park Mansions
Park Walk
London, SW10.

Dear Mr Seltzer,

Thank you for your letter of 7th June enclosing your letter of 5th June to Margaret, Duchess of Argyll, together with Ms Julia Mortimer's letters to the Duchess. I can now confirm that we would be delighted to act for you in the matter of Ms Mortimer's claim for 'wrongful dismissal'.

As I said on the telephone, the Duchess's evidence will be crucial so it is important that you should write to her seeking the name of her Solicitors so that we can serve the necessary papers on them, though this step could be avoided, of course, were the Duchess to write to you explaining her objections to Ms Mortimer's behaviour. I confirm that the fir hearing in front of the Industrial Relations Tribunal will at 10.30am at 93 Ebury Bridge Road, SW1, in front of Mr David Davies. It is necessary to get the Duchess to confir that she can attend with her solicitor.

Yours sincerely,

14ᵗʰ July

Copy sent to Duchess of Argyll 10/6/87

FILM AND TELEVISION COPYRIGHTS

139 Elm Park Mansions
Park Walk
London SW10

Tel: 01 – 352 9689
Telegrams: Concept London

Woman Detective Sergeant Wilson
Bow Street Police Station
Bow Street
London, WC2.

17th July 1987.

Dear Woman Detective Sergeant Wilson,

I am writing to you on behalf of our Executive Producer, Mr Aaron Seltzer (deceased) and can only say how astonished I am at this tasteless police intervention in his affairs at a time of great sorrow for his widow, his children and his mistress (our Miss Selina Sidey, who happened to be at his side in New York at the time of his mysterious accident. Miss Sidey herself merely has a small concussion, you will be glad to hear, and is expected back at her desk in the near future.)

That said, perhaps we can now talk business. Are you representing Margaret, Duchess of Argyll or is Mr Cobden Ramsey of Radcliffe & Co, who have recently put themselves forward as her theatrical agents?

If you, rather than Cobden Ramsey, are representing her, could you please let me know as soon as possible the answers to the questions put to her in our Miss Sidey's letter of 29th June. At the moment she is holding up shooting with her inability to make up her mind.

It occurs to me that the Duchess may not be the only artiste whom you represent. In case this is so, I now enclose a synopsis of CRACK-UP together with a full cast breakdown. We are still looking for an artiste to play the cabinet minister on the kebab skewer. Do you by any chance represent Edward Woodward?

To help you further with your casting suggestions, I also enclose a key scene, featuring Judge King-Hamilton QC, whom you'll remember well, I expect, from his days at the Old Baily. This will give you an idea, I think, of the strength and style of the series.

I look forward to hearing from you.

Yours sincerely,

Julia Mortimer

Julia Mortimer. Assistant Casting Director.

cc. Mr Cobden Ramsey, Radcliffe & Co, Theatrical Agents.

Jimmy Smits ~~Milton Goldfarb~~ ~~Alan Rachins~~ Daniel Ziskie ~~Aaron Seltzer~~ Sandy McPeak ~~Jill Eikenberry~~ ~~Jeremy Cox~~ ~~Angela Picano~~ ~~Max Templeton~~ Julia Mortimer

CRACK-UP. Episode 4. Scene 2. Interior. No 3 Court, The Old
Bailey. Present: JUDGE KING-HAMILTON QC, JANIE JONES (in the
dock), THE CLERK OF THE COURT, MEMBERS OF THE JURY, BARRISTERS,
REPORTERS and, in the public gallery, LORD 'A', LORD 'B', SIR 'C',
MR 'D', MR 'E', MR 'F', ADMIRAL 'G', 'DET-SUPT 'H', VISCOUNT 'I',
etc, who have all given evidence against her, as have - at the
other end of the public gallery - MISS 'S', MISS 'T', MISS 'U',
MISS 'V', MISS 'W', MISS 'X', MISS 'Y', and MISS 'Z'. The former
are wearing pin-stripe suits and Old Etonian ties, the latter are
in corsets and carrying bull-whips and fighting irons.

THE CLERK OF THE COURT (to the Jury): On the first charge of
blackmailing Lord 'A', Lord 'B' and Admiral 'G' - how say you?

THE FOREMAN OF THE JURY: Not guilty, me lud!

JUDGE KING-HAMILTON: Good God!

THE CLERK OF THE COURT: On the second charge of influencing the
movement of prostitutes, how say you?

THE FOREMAN OF THE JURY: Guilty, me lud!

JUDGE KING-HAMILTON: That's better! Miss so-called Jones, you
are without a doubt the most evil woman I have ever met. I
sentence you to be taken from this place and hanged by the neck
until.....

(THE CLERK OF THE COURT tugs at JUDGE KING-HAMILTON'S sleeve and
whispers in his ear.)

JUDGE KING-HAMILTON: Is that so? And more's the pity, that's all
I can say. Miss Jones, it seems that for the disgusting crime of
corrupting these innocent, naive women, who work, I have no doubt,
as secretaries at the BBC - (JUDGE KING-HAMILTON QC gestures towards
MISS 'X', MISS 'Y', MISS 'Z', etc, who are standing in the public
gallery leering and brandishing their fighting irons) - I must
sentence you to a lesser sentence than death by hanging. I
propose to send you to prison for seven years. Take the disgusting
woman down!

(JANIE JONES is led from the dock by a policewoman.)

MAX HASTINGS: Justice must tame whom mercy fails to train.

GEOFFREY WHEATCROFT: Ruat coelum, fiat justitia.

FADE.

CRACK-UP. Episode 4. Scene 3. Interior. The Dirty Duck, a pub
near The Old Bailey. Present: LORD 'A', LORD 'B', SIR 'C', MR 'D',
MR 'E', MR 'F', ADMIRAL 'G', DET-SUPT 'H', VISCOUNT 'I', etc, and
MISS 'S', MISS 'T', MISS 'U', MISS 'V', MISS 'W', MISS 'X', MISS 'Y'
and MISS 'Z' - the latter still in their corsets and brandishing
their bull-whips.

LORD 'B': Glad that's over. Good judge, King-Hamilton. Firm but
fair. Stern but stupid.

MISS 'W': One of the best.

MISS 'X': I don't know. She was acquitted, after all. Seven
years after you've been acquitted is a bit strong, isn't it?

ADMIRAL 'G': I tend to agree. Six years is about right for
something you haven't done. Seven was too much.

SIR 'C': Hear hear. Six years is reasonable when you've been
found not guilty.

MISS 'V': I think that's too much. Five would have been fair.

LORD 'B': Can't agree. Miss Jones was found not guilty of a
very serious crime. Let's not forget that. Seven years was
the right sentence in the circumstances. Still, I wouldn't like
to be in her place.

MISS 'Y': Nor would I. Let's go to yours.

LORD 'B': Good idea.

(LORD 'B' and MISS 'Y' get up and exit.)

MISS 'Z': Well, I'm off to see Lord Lambton.

MISS 'X': So am I. Come along Miss 'Z'.

RICHARD WEST: You can't legislate against human nature.

FADE.

From: Julia Mortimer.

To: Selina Sidey.

Date: 17th June.

Time: 11.55am.

Selina, love. Sara Randall called while you were having your hair done. Lynda Lee-Potter is keen to meet, and Sara suggests lunch on Wednesday 1st July. She'd prefer Odins to Langan's, because she's got to be in Baker Street in the afternoon. Shall I book?

Saraband Associates

265 Liverpool Road, Islington, London N1 1LX. Telephone: 01-609 5313/4
Sara Randall : Bryn Newton

Miss Selina Sidey,
139 Elm Park Mansions,
Park Walk,
London SW10

15th July 1987

Dear Selina,

A belated thank you for lunch.   It was really
nice to meet you.   As I am off to France on
Friday I thought I should drop you a line to say
is there any news on the situation?   I will be
seeing Lynda on 23rd July but then will be away
on holiday for a week so would be glad if you
would drop me a note or leave a message.

Many thanks,

Yours sincerely,

SARA RANDALL

Registered in England No. 1141148. Registered Office: Waterman House, Chertsey Road, Woking, Surrey.
Saraband Associates is the registered trade name of Shepherdswell Productions Limited
Directors: S. Randall : B. Newton : N. Smyth Employment Agents Act 1973 Licence No. SE(A)4080.
V.A.T. Registration No. 234 8538 48

Ms Lynda Lee-Potter
The Daily Mail
Carmelite House
London EC4Y OJA.

139 Elm Park Mansions
Park Walk
London SW10

Tel: 01 – 352 9689
Telegrams: Concept London

20th July 1987.

Dear Lynda,

It was just brilliant meeting you for lunch – though a little nerve-wracking too! I still go to pieces a bit when coming face to face with someone I particularly admire!

I now enclose some scenes from CRACK-UP, and apologise for the delay. I can hardly wait for your reaction! I just hope you're as excited by it as we all are. Working with you on it would be a real thrill!

It was sweet of you to ask me down for the weekend some time. It would be brilliant to get out of London for a bit, and I'll take you up on the offer really soon.

I look forward to hearing from you and to talking again.

With very best wishes.

Yours,

Selina Sidey.

FILM AND TELEVISION COPYRIGHTS

139 Elm Park Mansions
Park Walk
London SW10

Tel: 01 – 352 9689
Telegrams: Concept London

Mr R.A.M. Forrest
The Reform Club
Pall Mall
London, SW1Y 5EW.

23rd July 1987.

Dear Mr Forrest,

Many thanks for your letter of 17th July to Selina Sidey. Selina is suffering from a slight concussion at the moment so your letter has been passed over to me for PR action.

I have to tell you that it is too late to cancel our plans to shoot on your premises in the near future. We have already entered into binding agreements with Lady Geldof (Technical Adviser) and with Miss Jilly Johnson, the exciting young model, who, as you already know, will be playing the part of Lady Geldof in the shoot.

To discontinue our arrangements at the eleventh hour would involve us in a great deal of negative PR - much of which would inevitably drop on you - and a lot of costly litigation (Lady Geldof's affairs are in the hands of Mr Ed Victor, whose way of settling literary disputes is with an exchange of small arms fire).

In the circumstances, I have no option but to up the financial offer we made in our last letter. I am now authorised to bump this up to a flat sum of £25,000 (no points) for three days filming.

I look forward to receiving your confirmation that this offer is acceptable to you.

Yours sincerely,

Sandy McPeak. Publicity Director.

Ed Victor Ltd

Literary Agency

162 Wardour Street London W1V 3AT Telephone: 01-734 4795
Telex: 263361 Cables: Victorious London

27 July 1987

Ms Selina Sidey
FILM AND TELEVISION COPYRIGHTS
139 Elm Park Mansions
Park Walk
LONDON SW10

Dear Ms Sidey

Thank you for your letter of 23 July regarding Paula Yates and
your forthcoming television series CRACK-UP. I have sent your
letter on to Ms Yates and you will be hearing more on this
matter in due course.

In the meantime, we would like to see a copy of the script for
the scene involving Ms Yates and look forward to receiving this
from you soon.

Yours sincerely

Maggie Phillips
Assistant to Ed Victor

Directors: Ed Victor   Carol Ryan   Dasha Shenkman   Caroline Daubeny   Leon Morgan
Registered in England Registered Office: Regina House 124 Finchley Road London NW3 5JS
Registered Number 1270161 VAT Registration Number 234 9044 68

TELEPHONE:
01-930 9374.
(7 LINES)

PLEASE ADDRESS ALL
COMMUNICATIONS TO
THE SECRETARY

REFORM CLUB,

PALL MALL,

SWIY 5EW

27th. July, 1987.

Sandy McPeake, Esq.,
P.R. Director,
FILM and TELEVISION COPYRIGHTS,
139, Elm Park Mansions,
Park Walk,
LONDON.   S.W.10.

Dear Mr. McPeake,

I have received your letter of 23rd. July, 1987.

I do not think I can usefully add anything to what was said in my letter of 17th. July, 1987.   But in order that there may be no doubt about the matter let me make it clear that the Club has no interest in entering into any negotiations with you nor will it permit you to film in the Club.

Yours sincerely,

SECRETARY.
R.A.M.FORREST.

FILM AND TELEVISION COPYRIGHTS

139 Elm Park Mansions
Park Walk
London SW10

Tel: 01 – 352 9689
Telegrams: Concept London

31st July 1987.

Mr R.A.M. Forrest
Reform Club
Pall Mall
SW1 5EW.

Dear Mr Forrest,

Okay – you've got us by the balls, and I can't blame you for taking advantage of the situation. Nothing personal. I'd go for your balls were our positions reversed.

In these painful circumstances, I'm prepared to up our offer to £50,000 for three days shooting. I could also offer you an advisory role on the production team, which may be what you're holding out for. Let me know.

Might I ask you whether you were Club Secretary at the time of the original shoot? As the script for the scene stands at the moment, the Club Secretary is not named – but it has occurred to our author that if you were Club Secretary we could get some amusing word-play out of your initials! Would you object to this?

I would point out that I have no 'e' at the end of my name and find your insistence on putting one there highly offensive.

I look forward to hearing from you.

Yours sincerely,

Sandy McPeak. Publicity Director.

TELEPHONE:
01-930 9374.
(7 LINES)

PLEASE ADDRESS ALL
COMMUNICATIONS TO
THE SECRETARY

REFORM CLUB,

PALL MALL,

SWIY 5EW

3rd. August, 1987.

Sandy McPeak, Esq.,
P.R. Director,
FILM and TELEVISION COPYRIGHTS,
139, Elm Park Mansions,
Park Walk,
LONDON. S.W.10.

Dear Mr. McPeak,

I have your further letter of 31st. July, 1987.

We have made our position absolutely clear in my earlier
letters to you and I am afraid that we shall not be replying to
any further communication from you.

Yours sincerely,

SECRETARY.
R.A.M.FORREST.

FILM AND TELEVISION COPYRIGHTS

The Rt Hon Cecil Parkinson MP
The House of Commons
Westminster
London, SW1.

139 Elm Park Mansions
Park Walk
London SW10

Tel: 01 – 352 9689
Telegrams: Concept London

25th July 1987.

Dear Mr Parkinson,

I am surprised that I haven't had an answer yet to my letter of 24th June with regard to Mr Gerald Harper and Miss Stefanie Marrian playing the parts of yourself and Miss Sara Keays in CRACK-UP.

In fact we have now decided not to employ Miss Marrian after all. As you may have read in the press, she has recently 'embraced celibacy as the only viable option' and in the circumstances we think she might have a rather depressing effect on other members of the cast. Instead, we have offered the part of Miss Keays to Miss Jan Leeming - a more experienced actress than many people realise, and a woman who possesses much of Miss Keays's air of lethal vulnerability (aren't they the _end_, women like that?)

Quite frankly, your inability to answer my letters is holding up production and I must ask you to let us have your approval of these two artistes as soon as possible.

Yours sincerely,

Selina Sidey.   Casting Director.

International Management Group

Auckland · Boston · Cleveland · Geneva · Hong Kong · London · Los Angeles · Milan · Monte Carlo
Munich · New York · Paris · Perth · Rio de Janeiro · San Francisco · Sydney · Tokyo · Toronto
The Pier House · Strand on the Green · Chiswick · London W4 3NN · England · 01-994 1444 · Fax: 01-994 9606 · Telex: 267486

17th August 1987

Selina Sidey
Casting Director
Film and Television Copyrights
139 Elm Park Mansions
Park Walk
London SW10

Dear Selina,

Jan Leeming has asked me to write and thank you for your
letter concerning Crack-Up.

We really dont think this is quite right for Jan, but thank
you very much for thinking of her.

With best wishes.

Yours sincerely,

James Kelly

JK/mjo

International Management Group (U.K.) Inc.
(A Limited Liability Company Incorporated under the Laws of Ohio U.S.A.)
Directors: Mark H. McCormack (U.S.A.), Arthur J. Lafave Jr. (U.S.A.), William H. Carpenter (U.S.A.)
Associated Corporation: Trans World International (U.K.) Inc.
Registration Number in England F8032

FILM AND TELEVISION COPYRIGHTS

139 Elm Park Mansions
Park Walk
London SW10

Tel: 01 – 352 9689
Telegrams: Concept London

Mr David Vevers
Prudential Corporation
142 Holborn Bars
London EC1 2NH.

29th July 1987.

Dear David,

Thank you for your undated letter with reference to the scene in CRACK-UP featuring Mr F.B. Corby.

We have now merged this scene - quite adroitly, I think - with one featuring Lady Geldof's nude shoot at the Reform Club some years ago. I now enclose a copy, confident that when he has read it, Mr Corby will revise his decision not to appear in it as himself.

I very much look forward to hearing from you.

Yours sincerely,

Selina Sidey.

Selina Sidey. Casting Director.

Enc. CRACK-UP, Episode 8, Scene 7.

Jimmy Smits Milton Goldfarb

CRACK-UP. Episode 8. Scene 7. INTERIOR. The Reform Club, Pall Mall, London. Present: MISS PAULA ·YATES, MR BOB GELDOF, MR ROBIN SCHWARTZ (the photographer), MR R.A.M. FORREST (the Club Secretary), plus various BOGGLERS, CLUB MEMBERS, etc, (including MR F.B. CORBY, MR MAX HASTINGS, MR RICHARD WEST, MR GEOFFREY WHEATCROFT, etc). Time: early afternoon.

MR R.A.M. FORREST (greeting PAULA YATES, BOB GELDOF, SCHWARTZ, etc): How do you do? I'm R.A.M. Forrest, the Club Secretary.

PAULA YATES: Ooooh! You can butt my backside any time you like!

BOB GELDOF: Fockin' shot op, Paula.

PAULA YATES: Sorry, Bob.

MR R.A.M. FORREST: How do you do, Mr Geldof?

BOB GELDOF: Fock off.

MR R.A.M. FORREST: Oh. This way please.

(FORREST ushers them all into the members lounge, where a lot of old gentlemen are snoozing after lunch).

SCHWARTZ (the photographer): Okay Paula. Let's get on with it. Take your clothes off, if you would.

BOB GELDOF: Who the fock would want to see that?

PAULA YATES: Millions and millions of people, Bob. All the readers of Knave and.....

BOB GELDOF: Fockin' wankers.

PAULA YATES: But, Bob, you're always wan.....

BOB GELDOF: That's a'fockin' 'noff of that, Paula.

PAULA YATES: Sorry Bob.

BOB GELDOF: Let's get it fockin' over with.

FADE.

1st MEMBER: Jumping Jesus! What's that?

2nd MEMBER: What's what?

1st MEMBER: Over there. Straddling the bust of Gladstone. Never seen anything like that.

3rd MEMBER: Naked woman, is it?

2nd MEMBER: Good God I think it might be!

BARRY NORMAN: She's having a love-affair with the camera.

ANNA RAEBURN: Are you sure she isn't being sacrificed on the altar of our fantasies?

F.B. CORBY (waking up abruptly): Naked woman? Where? Where?

1st MEMBER: Over there, Corby. Upside down on the bust of Gladstone.

F.B. CORBY: Great heavens! How did she get into that position?

MAX HASTINGS: Acrobatics belong in the circus ring, not the bedroom.

RICHARD WEST: She must be French. We British understand that a shared sense of humour counts for more than expertise under the duvet.

F.B. CORBY: Nevertheless, it's given me a sound idea for the Pru's new advertising campaign! Fat little women with great big bosoms, that's the thing! 'Save with the Pru and in your dotage you'll be on your way to the Costa Del Sol with a car-load of bosomy bimbos!' I must go and ring my man Vevers! We'll audition at once!

(CORBY exits).

BOB GELDOF: Fockin' shot op over there! We're trying to do a fockin' shoot here!

GEOFFREY WHEATCROFT: As dear old Philip Larkin once said to me in the course of an agreeable stroll through a country churchyard - "Dear boy," he said, "in this sad life you must....."

BOB GELDOF: I thought I said fockin' shot op!

PAULA YATES: You must forgive them, Bob. It must be years since they saw unnecessary nudity and sex and violence and so on.

BOB GELDOF: Sex and fockin' violence? Same fockin' thing at their age, I suppose.

MAX HASTINGS: Four letter words are the sign of an impoverished vocabulary. That's what I always say.

GEOFFREY WHEATCROFT: Old Bill Shakespeare didn't need to use four letter words.

BERNARD LEVIN: Surely Bill Shakespeare was a conduit through whom God spoke to the world.

(Enter SELINA SIDEY, an astonishingly beautiful young woman in her

early twenties. Everyone gasps in amazement at her beauty, some
faint, others drop dead on the spot.)

BOB GELDOF: Fockin' hell!

GEOFFREY WHEATCROFT: She's the most beautiful girl I've ever
seen! I'm tired of mooching around in books and sitting on the
wrong end of my shooting-stick! I must follow her wherever she
goes!

(He approaches SELINA SIDEY).

GEOFFREY WHEATCROFT: Who are you?

SELINA SIDEY: My name is Selina Sidey. I am the astonishingly
beautiful Casting Director of CRACK-UP, a ten-part television
drama/documentary currently being developed by Film and Television
Copyrights. Why don't you join us as my assistant and Head of
our Publishing Division?

GEOFFREY WHEATCROFT: My word, I think I will.

(Exit SELINA SIDEY followed by GEOFFREY WHEATCROFT).

FADE.

FILM AND TELEVISION COPYRIGHTS

139 Elm Park Mansions
Park Walk
London SW10

Nick Chapman Esq
Editorial Director
BBC Publications
35 Marylebone High Street
London, W1.

Tel: 01 – 352 9689
Telegrams: Concept London

30th July 1987.

Dear Nick,

    Surely it was dear old Jamie Hamilton who said 'When one tires of publishing parties, one tires of - well - publishing parties'? Delightful! After years of mooching about in the book trade, combined with a bit of agreeable journalism, I have decided to accept a somewhat livelier role with this conglomorate.

    <u>A</u> <u>notres</u> <u>moutons</u>, as Flaubert surely said! I gather that you are bringing out 'Hullo Hullo' by Jimmy Riddle in time for Christmas '88, so you're not averse to a squalid idea with publishing potential.

    Here's another which might be of interest. We are, as you will have already heard, mounting a ten-part TV series starring Sir John Gielgud, Anthony Andrews, Margaret, Duchess of Argyll, Cecil Parkinson, Lindy Benson and heaven knows who else, all under the agreeable direction of Lindsey Anderson.

    I now enclose some scenes together with some press coverage we have received and suggest that you publish the book of the series - CRACK-UP by Norman Smallhampton, a novel. Why? Because we'll see to it that it wins the Booker Prize!

    Here's how: I have already been on to Ladbrokes and William Hill, asking them what odds I could get against Smallhampton winning. Once they had discovered that he had never written a novel - indeed that he had never written anything - Ladbrokes offered me 2000 to 1 against and William Hill 1500 to 1. We place £10,000 on Smallhampton to win the Booker Prize and I don't have to tell you what we trouser when he does - which he will, of course, because we have £3½ million guranteed with which to 'influence' the judges!

    What do you say? Are you <u>pour</u> <u>ou</u> <u>contre</u>?

Yours sincerely,

G. Wheatcroft. Publishing Division.

TELEPHONE 01 601 2222

EXT 2220
TELEGRAMS ADJUTOR LONDON TELEX

CITY OF LONDON POLICE,

26, OLD JEWRY,

LONDON, EC2R 8DJ.

OFFICIAL LETTERS TO BE ADDRESSED :-
THE COMMISSIONER OF POLICE
FOR THE CITY OF LONDON.

PLEASE QUOTE REF. A12/59/87

YOUR REF.

28th July, 1987.

Dear Sir,

With reference to your letter dated 26th
May, 1987, I have been directed by the Commissioner of
Police for the City of London to inform you that he must
decline your kind offer to appear in the "Crack-up" series.

Regarding permission to film in the street,
please continue to liaise with Chief Superintendent 'A'
Department and his Functions Officer.

Yours faithfully,

J.R. WILSON - Chief Inspector
(Media Liaison Officer)

Mr. Daniel Ziskie,
Executive Editor,
Film and Television Copyrights,
139, Elm Park Mansions,
Park Walk,
LONDON S.W.10.

FILM AND TELEVISION COPYRIGHTS

139 Elm Park Mansions
Park Walk
London SW10

Tel: 01 – 352 9689
Telegrams: Concept London

Chief Inspector J.R. Wilson
Media Liason Officer
City of London Police
London EC2R 8DJ.

31st July 1987.

Dear Chief Inspector Wilson,

Many thanks for your letter of 28th July. We are disappointed, of course, by the Commissioner's last minute decision not to
appear in CRACK-UP by HENRY ROOT ('A Nation In The Dock!') but I
do not suppose that his refusal to be quizzed on camera will look
in any way suspicious. We will certainly do nothing to encourage
the viewing public to leap to that conclusion. You have my word
on that. That said - could we now have the Commissioner's permission to issue a press release concerning his reluctance to put
his head above the parapet?

With regard to filming in the street, you say in your letter
that we should continue to liase with Chief Superintendant A. Department and his functions officer. In fact we have been liasing
with Chief Superintendant Cardwell, who we now realise is the
wrong man. However, when we rang up Wood Street nick asking to
speak to Superintendant Department they said there was no such
person!

I would be most grateful if you could tell us whom exactly
we should be dealing with. As things are I'm beginning to think
we should retitle the series COCK-UP!

Finally, are you by any chance of the same family business
as Woman Detective Sergeant Wilson of the Bow Street Police? If
you are, you will know that she has recently put herself forward
as Margaret, Duchess of Argyll's sole representative in theatrical
matters. Thinking she must represent other artistes, we sent her
a cast breakdown of CRACK-UP, but she has not so far come up with
any suggestions. We are still looking for someone to play the
Cabinet Minister on the kebab skewer. Could you tell her this when
you next see her?

Please excuse the smell of herrings - I'm afraid I bought my
dinner on the way to the Post Office.

Yours sincerely,

Daniel Ziskie. Producer.

OPPENHEIMERS

HERBERT OPPENHEIMER, NATHAN & VANDYK

20 COPTHALL AVENUE LONDON EC2R 7JH
TEL: 01-628 9611 TELEX: 885240 CLIENT G
FACSIMILE: 01-638 2084 01-628 4729 LDE/CDE: 123

WILLIAM M. PYBUS	JUDITH PORTRAIT	ASSOCIATES
PETER G. NATHAN	COLIN BAMFORD	
PETER W. SUMMERFIELD	MONICA A. BLAKE	G. D. HARRIS
DIANA J. COURTNEY	K. G. OLLERTON	BRYAN J. PICKUP
F. J. DONAGH	MARK WENBORN	A. L. HUMPHREY
BRIAN EAGLES	C. I. M. LESLIE	HELEN NORRIS
COLIN L. CORK	CHRISTINE J. WILLIAMS	IAN AIREY
I. MESHOULAM	PENELOPE A. DAVIES	DAVID G. HUGHES
J. M. OSLER	JOHN W. GARNER	MARTIN QUICKE
JOHN ROSENHEIM	A. P. SCOTT	N. B. STRAW
PETER J. N. PRESLAND	ALAN JARVIS	MOIRA BUTCHER
J. H. SURGEONER	JENNIFER PALMER	GARY GRAVES
ANTHONY E. ALEXANDER	DAVID MILES	NIGEL MILLER
R. D. FOX	STEVEN BLAKELEY	STELLA HOLT
G. M. TISDALL		STEVEN F. LOBLE

CONSULTANT: LORD NATHAN

OUR REFERENCE   YOUR REFERENCE

BE/18.98/yy   28th July 1987

Daniel Ziskie, Esq.,
Film and Television Copyrights,
139 Elm Park Mansions,
Park Walk,
London SW10

Dear Mr. Ziskie,

"Crack-up"

I represent Mandy Rice-Davies who has instructed me in connection with
your above project.   Ms. Rice-Davies has also sent to me copies of
correspondence from you and others of your partnership to her Agent,
Mr. Vincent Shaw.

So that I can advise my Client more fully in connection with this matter
it would be helpful, if your team of writers are back from their
re-writing exercise in the South of France, if the three other important
scenes to which Selina Sidey refers in her letter of the 3rd June could
be sent to me for consideration.

Yours sincerely,

Brian Eagles

FILM AND TELEVISION COPYRIGHTS

139 Elm Park Mansions
Park Walk
London SW10

Tel: 01 – 352 9689
Telegrams: Concept London

Mr Brian Eagles
Oppenheimers
20 Copthall Avenue
London EC2R 7JH.

31st July 1987.

Dear Mr Eagles,

Thank you for your letter of 28th July in the matter re your client Miss Mandy Rice-Davies and our TV series CRACK-UP.

I now enclose the scenes you ask for and would advise you that we ourselves are represented in re this matter by Lord Mishcon no less. Incidentally, when I mentioned you to him he remarked: 'Ah – he'll be one of the legal Eagles'. I thought that was rather good, but I expect you've heard it before.

I wonder whether you represent any other artistes who might be of use to us. Our Casting Director, Selina Sidey, has asked me to tell you that we are still searching for someone to play the cabinet minister on the kebab skewer (see Episode 2, Scene 8, enclosed). Do you by any chance represent Donald Sinden?

I look forward to hearing from you.

Yours sincerely,

Daniel Ziskie. Producer.

PS. Kindly return the enclosed pages having perused in re a tort.

OPPENHEIMERS

HERBERT OPPENHEIMER, NATHAN & VANDYK

20 COPTHALL AVENUE LONDON EC2R 7JH
TEL: 01-628 9611 TELEX: 885240 CLIENT G
FACSIMILE: 01-638 2084 01-628 4729 LDE/CDE: 123

4th August 1987

YOUR REFERENCE

OUR REFERENCE
BE/18.140/yy

Daniel Ziskie, Esq.,
Film and Television Copyrights,
139 Elm Park Mansions,
Park Walk,
London SW10

Dear Mr. Ziskie,

Re: "Crack-Up"

Thank you for your letter of the 31st July and for your courtesy in
sending me the several pages of script concerned. I note the defensive
stance which you adopt and, having taken copies, return the pages as
requested.

I am very surprised at the remark attributed to Lord Mishcon because
he knows that I am the "legal eagle". You are quite correct, I have
indeed heard the remark before and I do not think it particularly
funny - but then, perhaps, the joke is on you!

Yours sincerely,

Brian Eagles

Jimmy Smits Mr

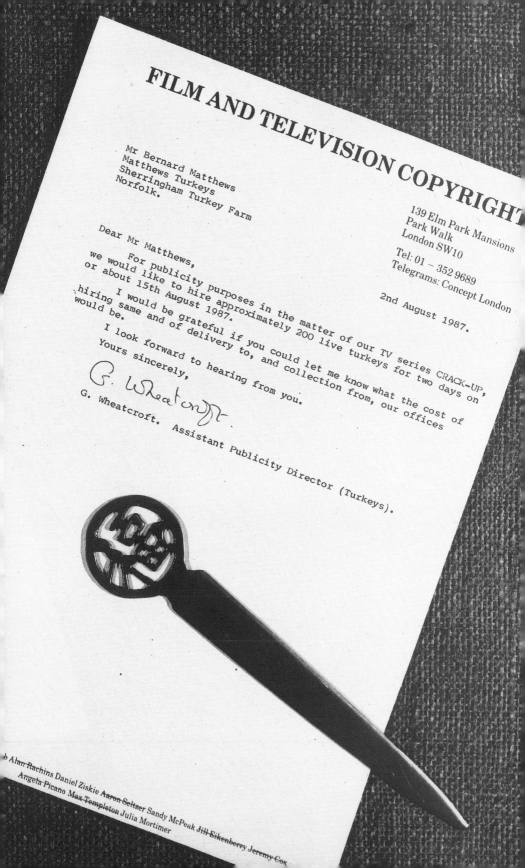

FILM AND TELEVISION COPYRIGHT

Mr Bernard Matthews
Matthews Turkeys
Sherringham Turkey Farm
Norfolk.

139 Elm Park Mansions
Park Walk
London SW10
Tel: 01 – 352 9689
Telegrams: Concept London

2nd August 1987.

Dear Mr Matthews,

For publicity purposes in the matter of our TV series CRACK-UP, we would like to hire approximately 200 live turkeys for two days on or about 15th August 1987.

I would be grateful if you could let me know what the cost of hiring same and of delivery to, and collection from, our offices would be.

I look forward to hearing from you.

Yours sincerely,

G. Wheatcroft

G. Wheatcroft. Assistant Publicity Director (Turkeys).

b Alan Rachins Daniel Ziskie Aaron Seltzer Sandy McPeak Jill Eikenberry Jeremy Cox
Angela Picano Max Templeton Julia Mortimer

For the next three years Fergie enjoyed the life of private jets and Grand Prix, of winters skiing and summers lying by a pool in Ibiza, where Paddy had a villa half a mile away from Niki Lauda's. Friends expected the happy-go-lucky couple to get married but the affair came to an end for Sarah as suddenly as it had begun. Italian banker's son Giorgio Paulli, who has lived in Ibiza since 1967, remembers the occasion well.

'It happened at a lunch party given by Michael Pearson. Sarah suddenly stood up and said, "This is leading nowhere! I'm off!" And she walked out. We never saw her again.'

'Typical of Fergie,' says another close friend, Lulu Blackwater. 'She was suddenly tired of always being 20 years younger than anyone else in the room. Paddy's charming, but his friends are all old phoneys and geriatric playboys like that frightful little man Taki. Fergie wanted to settle down and have children. I think Paddy was good for her, though. He taught her a lot. In a way he was her Koo Stark.'

In 1984, a man from Leicester put a £50 bet on at Ladbrokes that the christian name of Amorous Andy's next girlfriend would end with an 'i'. The following week, the *Daily Mail* revealed the latest 'raunchy romance of the Romeo Prince – Sandi Jones' – and the lucky punter cleaned up!

Fact: Over 50 per cent of the royal heart-throb's flings have been with girls whose names end with an 'i'.

Stagestruck Sarah's favourite actress is comedienne Felicity Kendal, whom she names as the person she would most like to be if she couldn't be herself. 'I just adore her bubbly sense of fun and the amazingly funny faces she's always pulling!'

It is, in fact, a royal beauty secret that animated Fergie practises Felicity Kendal expressions in the mirror each morning, pulling faces and rolling her eyes – her best features.

Royal beauty secret. Fergie learnt early in life that it's 'P for Personality' that counts! An admirer of TV funny girl Felicity Kendal's bubbly sense of fun, she practises zany expressions in front of the mirror every morning.

'Let's face it, Sarah saw things in Ibiza she didn't like,' says Jo Bassett-Turner, a former girlfriend of Jamie, the Marquis of Blandford. 'They're all quite mad out there and on drugs most of the time. Fergie hated all that. She's absolutely genuine, if you know what I mean; what a racehorse trainer would call "honest". Some of the parties were quite wild. She told me about one to which all the men had to come as Adolf Hitler and all the girls as Eva Braun. The party went on all night and at breakfast time they all staggered into Ibiza Town as high as kites. When the local police saw 30 Adolf Hitlers having coffee outside the Montesol they called the German Consul, who had a nervous breakdown.'

Feet-on-the-ground Fergie had seen enough. She packed her bags that morning and flew to London. The incident left her with an abiding hatred of drugs.

'Mind you,' says Jo, 'she's stood by Jamie through all his troubles. That's typical of her. She's one of the few friends he's got. She visits him in prison, in the clinic, on parole, on probation, on remand, on the run – wherever he happens to be at the time.'

The Ferguson family has never believed in the concept of the 'generation gap'. The royal bride's stepmother Sue – Major Ronnie Ferguson's second wife – is a youthful 39. Had Paddy McNally married Sarah, his mother-in-law would have been nine years younger than he was!

FILM AND TELEVISION COPYRIGHTS

139 Elm Park Mansions
Park Walk
London SW10

Tel: 01 – 352 9689
Telegrams: Concept London

Mrs Ros Chatto,
Chatto and Linnet Ltd
Prince of Wales Theatre
Coventry Street
London W1V 7FE.

3rd August 1987.

My dear Mrs Chatto,

As you will know, this company is shortly to go into production with CRACK-UP, a ten-part TV series dealing with the moral collapse of this once great country.

One of our subjects will be the changing behaviour patterns of the younger Royals. We have recently acquired worldwide rights from Pan in '101 THINGS YOU DIDN'T KNOW ABOUT THE ROYAL LOVEBIRDS' by Talbot Church. We will be dramatising the enclosed episode from this book, featuring Sarah Ferguson in Ibiza, and now wonder whether your artiste Miss Felicity Kendal would like to play the part of Sarah in this scene.

We would like to shoot it in Ibiza before the end of the season (the middle of October), so if Felicity is available perhaps you could let me know and I will forward a script immediatey.

As you obviously know, Felicity is the Duchess of York's favourite actress, so who better to play her in our series?

With best wishes.

Yours sincerely,

G. Wheatcroft

G. Wheatcroft. Assistant to the Assistant Casting Director.

CRACK-UP. Inter-Office Information Memo.

Date: 5th August.
Time: 12.10pm.

ZISKIE to WHEATCROFT.

While you were out, a Mrs Ros Chatto phoned about Felicity Kendal.
She's pregnant.

Date: 5th August.
Time: 3.30pm.

WHEATCROFT to ZISKIE.

Ros Chatto pregnant? Whatever next?

Date: 5th August.
Time: 5.35.

ZISKIE to WHEATCROFT.

Not Ros Chatto, you beanbag, Felicity Kendal. Try for that fat girl
in Coronation Street.

Penguin Books Ltd

27 Wrights Lane
London W8 5TZ

Telephone 01 938 2200
Telex 917181/2
Fax 01 937 8704

Daniel Ztisky
Film and Television Copyrights
139 Elm Park Mansions
Park Walk
London SW10

3 August 1987

Dear Daniel Ztisky (or should I call you Geoffrey?)

As one of the people responsible for the book ENTERTAINING AT HOME
by Cynthia Payne (101 PARTY HINTS BY BRITAIN'S MOST POPULAR HOSTESS),
your fascinating proposal has landed on my desk.

Though I am not sure how easy it would be to corrupt P D James,
I find the moral stand Mr Smallhampton is making most encouraging.
Would you like to come round and tell me more about it?

Yours sincerely,

Tim Binding
Chief Editor

FILM AND TELEVISION COPYRIGHTS

139 Elm Park Mansions
Park Walk
London SW10

Tel: 01 – 352 9689
Telegrams: Concept London

Mr Bernard Matthews
Matthews Turkeys
Sherringham Turkey Farm
Norfolk.

5th August 1987.

Dear Mr Matthews,

    Further to our telephone conversation of yesterday's date, I understand that it is not your policy to hire turkeys – rather that we would have to purchase them outright.

    The price of £6 per turkey, including delivery of same to our office, is acceptable to us, and I now enclose our cheque for £1200 and look forward to the arrival of the turkeys on the morning of 12th August.

    Yours sincerely,

G. Wheatcroft

G. Wheatcroft. Assistant Publicity Director (Turkeys).

PETER CARTER-RUCK AND PARTNERS

SOLICITORS
PRIVY COUNCIL AGENTS

PETER F. CARTER-RUCK
JOHN H. W. NEWMAN
MALCOLM B. CUTTLE
JULIE SCOTT-BAYFIELD
GEORGE W. J. BRIDGE
NEVILLE A. ROWLES
ALASTAIR R. NEALE
D. E. F. CLIFFORD
ALASTAIR K. MAXWELL
THE HON. FIONA JACK
BRIAN J. HEPWORTH
ELIZABETH A. WILDING
RICHARD G. WILLIAMSON
ANDREW STEPHENSON
ALASDAIR G. T. PEPPER

CONSULTANT
CHARLES B. BAINES M.B.E.

ASSOCIATES
NORMAN MACLEOD
ADMITTED IN CALIFORNIA
MARK LAMBERT
ANNE-MARIE PAGETT
PAUL FOX

ESSEX HOUSE
ESSEX STREET
STRAND
LONDON WC2R 3AH
AND
70/71 NEW BOND STREET
LONDON W1

TEL. 01 379 3456
TELEX. 265277 Libel G.
CABLES. Libel London WC2
FAX. 01 240 1486
DX 333

PFCR/SEJ

6 August 1987

Ms Selina Sidey
Film and Television Copyrights
139 Elm Park Mansions
Park Walk
LONDON
SW10

Dear Madam

Your letter to our client, Rt. Hon. Cecil Parkinson MP, dated 25 July has been passed on to us by him for attention on his behalf.

Our client does not have a copy of your letter of 24 June to which you refer and we should accordingly be grateful if you would kindly let us have a copy of that letter, on receipt of which we shall be in a position to advise our client.

Yours faithfully

Peter Carter-Ruck and Partners

SAN FRANCISCO
182 2nd Street
4th Floor
415 362 4000

PARIS
1 Avenue du
President Wilson
720 85 49

MANCHESTER
Orient House, Granby Row
061 236 3234

HONG KONG
5 Queens Road Central
852 5 210 3238

JERSEY C.I.
La Falaise Gorey Hill
0534 55329

GLASGOW
136 West George St.
041 331 1401

FILM AND TELEVISION COPYRIGHTS

139 Elm Park Mansions
Park Walk
London SW10

Tel: 01 – 352 9689
Telegrams: Concept London

7th August 1987.

Peter Carter-Ruck And Partners
Essex House
Essex Street
Strand
London WC2R 3AH.

Dear Sir or Madam,

Thank you for your letter of 6th August in re the matter of Cecil Parkinson MP's appearance in our TV series CRACK-UP.

As I said to him in my letter of 25th July, he is now holding up shooting with his inability to make up his mind, so I man delighted that he has now put his career in the hands of professionals.

I enclose a copy of my letter of 24th June, as requested, and would be grateful for Mr Parkinson's decision as soon as possible, since we plan to shoot his scene early next month.

Meanwhile, I enclose a complete cast break-down of the series in the hope that you may represent other artistes suitable for smaller parts. We're having <u>terrible</u> trouble finding someone to play the Cabinet Minister on the kebab skewer. Do you by any chance represent Simon Callow?

Yours sincerely,

Selina Sidey. Casting Director.

FILM AND TELEVISION COPYRIGHTS

139 Elm Park Mansions
Park Walk
London SW10

Tel: 01 – 352 9689
Telegrams: Concept London

Assistant Commissioner Somerset Ogden
Metropolitan Police
New Scotland Yard
Broadway
London SW1H OBG.

11th August 1987.

Dear Mr Ogden,

You will recall that I wrote to you on 3rd June 1987 seeking permission for Detective Superintendent Penrose to play himself in a scene from our TV series CRACK-UP featuring a front-page drugs bust involving that disgusting young man, the Marquis of Beauchamp. You were unable to help us on that occasion, but two other matters have arisen on which you may be able to help us.

1. Dealing with sensitive matters as we have been, we sent certain material to the Chairman of Harrods on 26th May for deposit in a security box. We received no acknowledgement of the safe arrival of this material, and subsequent letters to Harrods have gone unanswered. It now looks as if Harrods has simply 'stolen' this sensitive material as arrogantly as if two of their 'plumbers' had been through our office disguised as a poacher's pocket. Here's my question. Is this a matter for the police, and which branch of the police should I contact for the issuing of a prosecution?

B. Our Assistant PR Director (Turkeys), Mr Wheatcroft, recently had a good idea for publicising our series. He has bought several hundredweight of live turkeys from Mr Bernard Matthews's Norfolk Turkey Farm for the dropping from light aircraft over the City of London while filming inside Morgan Grenfell plc's 'Powder Room'.

Exercise Live Turkey is scheduled for 18th August. Each turkey will have a rosette pinned to its chest marked 'TURKEYS SUPPORT CRACK-UP!' and I would be grateful if you could let me know whether there are any laws extant or otherwise restricting the dropping of live turkeys over Morgan Grenfell plc for PR purposes?

I look forward to hearing from you.

Yours sincerely,

Daniel Ziskie. Producer.

TELEPHONE. 01 601 2222

EXT

TELEGRAMS ADJUTOR LONDON. TELEX

OFFICIAL LETTERS TO BE ADDRESSED:-
THE COMMISSIONER OF POLICE
FOR THE CITY OF LONDON.

PLEASE QUOTE REF.   A12/59/87

YOUR REF.

CITY OF LONDON POLICE,

26, OLD JEWRY,

LONDON, EC2R 8DJ.

5th August, 1987.

Dear Mr. Ziskie,

I am in receipt of your letter dated 31st July concerning the television series entitled CRACK-UP.

Chief Inspector Wilson is currently on holiday and as his deputy I have noted your comments in respect of the letter he forwarded to you on 28th July. It is a matter for you to decide upon the necessity and content for any press release you may wish to publish.

With regard to your proposal to film in the City streets, I would reiterate the information supplied by Chief Inspector Wilson that you continue to liaise with the Chief Superintendent 'A' DEPARTMENT, whose deputy is Superintendent Cardwell with whom you have been corresponding throughout in this matter.

Yours sincerely,

J.C. NOTTON - Inspector
Staff Officer.

Mr. Daniel Ziskie,
Executive Editor,
Film and Television Copyrights,
139, Elm Park Mansions,
Park Walk,
LONDON S.W.10.

Inspector J.C. Notton
City of London Police
26 Old Jewry
London EC2R 8DJ.

139 Elm Park Mansions
Park Walk
London SW10

Tel: 01 – 352 9689
Telegrams: Concept London

12th August 1987.

Dear Inspector Notton,

Thank you for your kind letter of 5th August concerning our
TV series CRACK-UP and our plans to film in the City of London in
the near future.

I will, as you suggest, continue to liase with Chief Superintendent Department - in spite of the fact that no one's heard of
him.

Do you happen to know anything about turkeys? We have recently taken on a Mr G. Wheatcroft.

Yours sincerely,

Daniel Ziskie. Producer.

FILM AND TELEVISION COPYRIGHTS

139 Elm Park Mansions
Park Walk
London SW10

Tel: 01 – 352 9689
Telegrams: Concept London

The Publicity Director
Morgan Grenfell & Co Ltd
23 Winchester Street
London, EC2.

12th August 1987.

Dear Sir or Madam,

As you will have heard from Superintendent Department of the
City Police, we will be filming certain scenes from CRACK-UP in the
environs of Great Winchester Street on Tuesday 18th August from
7am to 6pm.

I suggest that we come to some mutually beneficial arrangement
whereby we film two scenes on your premises - one partaking of your
entrance and main hall, the other of your gentleman's lavatory (or
Powder Room).

We would pay a nominal sum for this privilege, of course, but
I would stress the excellent PR which would accrue to you from our
filming. It would be of some assistance to us were certain of your
management staff and others to go about their normal business on
camera (visits to the 'Powder Room' etc) and to this end I would be
grateful if you could put a copy of this letter on your staff notice-
board, seeking volunteers to act as unpaid extras - chinless eggs in
butcher-stripe shirts, sharp-faced girls on £150,000 per annum plus
Porsche etc.

Please further note that two hundred live turkeys will be
dropped over Morgan Grenfell plc from light aircraft between 2.30
and 3.30 in the pm.

I look forward to hearing from you.

Yours sincerely,

G. Wheatcroft. Assistant Publicity Director (Turkeys).

METROPOLITAN POLICE OFFICE

NEW SCOTLAND YARD
BROADWAY LONDON SW1H 0BG
Telephone 01—230 1212 Extn.

Mr D Ziskie
Film & Television Copyrights
139 Elm Park Mansions
Park Walk
LONDON SW10

Your ref.:

Our ref.:

26ᵗʰ August 1987

Form 7110

Dear Mr Ziskie

Thank you for your letter dated August 11. With reference to your complaint against Harrods; should you wish to take this any further, I would suggest that you contact Kensington police station, who may be able to offer advice.

As regards your question concerning the dropping of live turkeys from a light aircraft, there is indeed an extant law which prohibits this. The law in question is the Air Navigation Order (1985), section 40, subsection 1, which states "articles and animals (whether or not attached to parachutes) shall not be dropped, or permitted to drop, from an aircraft in flight so as to endanger persons or property." I would also point out that you would be liable to prosecution by the RSPCA, since turkeys are flightless birds, and the experience of being dropped from a height is likely to prove fatal to them.

I hope that this information will be of use to you.

Yours sincerely

Miss J Clark
Information Officer
Broadcast Group
Directorate of Public Affairs

FILM AND TELEVISION COPYRIGHTS

139 Elm Park Mansions
Park Walk
London SW10

Tel: 01 – 352 9689
Telegrams: Concept London

Miss J. Clark
Information Officer
Broadcast Group
Directorate of Public Affairs
New Scotland Yard
Broadway
London SW1H OBG.

27th August 1987.

Dear Miss Clark,

Don't tell us! Between the hours of 2.30 and 3.30 on the afternoon of 18th August, two hundred turkeys fell out of the sky like sacks of cement on to the heads of Morgan Grenfell employees, not least Sir Peter Carey himself.

Thirty-eight people were taken to hospital and all the executives of this company were arrested by Superintendent Department of the City Police, with the exception of myself and Miss Selina Sidey. Miss Sidey turns out to have friends at Scotland Yard (do you know a Detective Superintendent Lundy?) and I evaded arrest by wearing a bowler hat abd standing under a turkey as a City commuter. I was myself unconscious for six hours, this accounting for my column in the Sunday Telegraph last week.

The series CRACK-UP is now as dead as the turkeys and after an agreeable break strolling round the Dordogne in search of a St Emilion '76 I will have to return to mooching around in books.

Yours sincerely,

G. Wheatcroft. Formerly Assistant PR Director (Turkeys).

BBC ENTERPRISES

Woodlands 30 Wood Lane London W12 0TT Telephone 01 743 5588 & 01 576 0202 Telex 934678 & 265781 Cables: Telecentre London

BOOKS

Extension 2630

15350/SA/sds

14 September 1987

G. Wheatcroft
Publishing Division
Film and Television Copyright
139 Elm Park Mansions
Park Walk
London SW10

Dear Mr Wheatcroft,

I have tried ringing you on a half dozen occasions to talk to you about 'Crack-Up',
but without success. Could you ring me on 576 0630?

Has the series been sold to the BBC? The press material you sent me mentions
Channel 4.

With best wishes,

Yours sincerely,

Sheila Ableman
Senior Commissioning Editor

BBC ENTERPRISES

BBC Enterprises Limited is a subsidiary of the British Broadcasting Corporation

Registered Number: 1420078 England Registered Office Woodlands 80 Wood Lane London W12 0TT

The Martha & Luke Home For Distressed Old Folk

123 Cedar Avenue

Budleigh-Salterton

Devon.

Mr Henry Root
139 Elm Park Mansions
Park Walk
London, SW10.   1st September 1987.

Dear Mr Root,

As you can see, poor Mabel and I finally lost our beloved
Rosewood Cottage and have ended up in this rather unhappy place.
Still, we mustn't grumble, I suppose. At least we're still together,
and I'm still scribbling!

You were so helpful to me with my silly television play, and
I wonder if you've had time to read it yet? I sent you my only copy,
you know, so if you could possibly let me have it back, I'd be so
very grateful.

I do so hope that you and yours are prospering as well as we can
hope to in this rather sad old world!

Yours ever,

Lucy Appleby.

The Receiver
Film & Television Copyrights (in liquidation)
I39 Elm Park Mansions
Park Walk
London, SWIO.

Ist October I987.

Dear Sir,

    I would be grateful if you could give me any information you may have on the current whereabouts of the below specified executives of the above company (in liquidation).

    Mr Jimmy Smits
    Mr Milton Goldfarb (deceased).
    Mr Alan Rachins
    Mr Daniel Ziskie
    Mr Aaron Seltzer (believed deceased).
    Mr Sandy McPeak
    Mr G. Wheatcroft (believed concussed).
    Mr Jeremy Cox (possibly an alias)
    Miss Angelo Picano
    Miss Julia Mortimer
    Mr Max Templeton (possibly an alias).

    All are wanted in connection with enquiries I am carrying out into acts of fraud, criminal libel, deception and forgery (letters from the Pope, the Home Office, Oswald Hickson, Collier & Co - solicitors) perpetrated by officers of the company.

    I would be grateful if you could get in touch with me at your earliest convenience.

    Yours faithfully,

Nigel Virgo. Detective Inspector (Fraud Squad).